Ben Hufford

PENGUIN BOOKS

TRAVELS WITH EPICURUS

Daniel Klein is the author, along with Thomas Cathcart, of the international bestseller *Plato and a Platypus Walk into a Bar . . .* and *Heidegger and a Hippo Walk Through Those Pearly Gates*. A graduate of Harvard with a degree in philosophy, he is the author or coauthor of twenty-five other books. He lives in western Massachusetts with his wife, Freke Vuijst.

—⁓—

An insightful meditation." —*The New York Times Book Review*

"Along the way, Klein touches on the ideas of Bertrand Russell, Erik Erikson, Aristotle, and William James. Klein's narrative is a delightful and spirited conversation, offering up the ingredients inherent to the art of living well in old age." —*Publishers Weekly*

"Charming and accessible, this philosophical survey simply and accessibly makes academic philosophy relevant to ordinary human emotion." —*Kirkus Reviews*

"Witty and wry." —*The Huffington Post*

"A lovely little book with both heart and punch." —*Booklist*

"A charming meditation on aging. Daniel Klein takes us on a thought-provoking journey." —*The Weekly Standard Book Review*

"Reading this book after a period of overwork and high stress, I was bowled over by its easy charm and hard-won wisdom. I shall be buying it in bulk as presents for my equally overburdened peers, and I suspect a few older people will enjoy it, too."
—Markus Berkmann, *The Daily Mail* (London)

"If you think philosophy is hard stuff that makes your head spin and possibly hurt, Klein is the perfect guide to deep thinking. Being fully aware and wondering how best to spend our time are useful practices at any age, and this warm, thought-provoking book is a terrific introduction to thinking about life philosophically."
—*Concord Monitor*

Travels with Epicurus

A JOURNEY TO A GREEK ISLAND

IN SEARCH OF A FULFILLED LIFE

DANIEL KLEIN

PENGUIN BOOKS

PENGUIN BOOKS

Published by the Penguin Group
Penguin Group (USA) LLC
375 Hudson Street
New York, New York 10014

USA | Canada | UK | Ireland | Australia | New Zealand | India | South Africa | China
penguin.com
A Penguin Random House Company

First published in the United States of America by Penguin Books 2012
This paperback edition published 2014

Grateful acknowledgment is made for permission to reprint excerpts from the following copyrighted
works:

"I Get a Kick Out of You" (from "Anything Goes"), words and music by Cole Porter. Copyright ©
1934 (renewed) WB Music Corp. All rights reserved. Used by permission.

"I See It Now," words by William Engvick, music by Alec Wilder. Published by TRO – © Copyright
1964 (renewed) Ludlow Music, Inc., New York, New York. International copyright secured. Made in
U.S.A. All rights reserved including public performance for profit. Used by permission.

"Once Upon A Time" by Charles Strouse and Lee Adams. Copyright © 1962 by Charles Strouse and
Lee Adams. Copyright renewed. International copyright secured. All rights reserved. Used by permission of Williamson Music, a division of Rodgers & Hammerstein: An Imagem Company.

"This Is All I Ask," words and music by Gordon Jenkins. Copyright © 1958 (renewed) Chappell &
Co., Inc. (ASCAP) and EMI Robbins Catalog Inc. (ASCAP). All rights reserved. Used by permission.

"Why Should Not Old Men Be Mad?" from *The Collected Works of W. B. Yeats, Volume 1: The Poems*,
revised, edited by Richard J. Finneran. Copyright © 1940 by Georgie Yeats, renewed 1968 by Bertha
Georgie Yeats, Michael Butler Yeats, and Anne Yeats. All rights reserved. Reprinted with permission
of Scribner, a division of Simon & Schuster, Inc.

THE LIBRARY OF CONGRESS HAS CATALOGED THE HARDCOVER EDITION AS FOLLOWS:
Klein, Daniel M.
Travels with Epicurus : a journey to a Greek island in search of a fulfilled life / Daniel Klein.
p. cm.
ISBN 978-0-14-312193-0 (hc.)
ISBN 978-0-14-312662-1 (pbk.)
1. Epicureans (Greek philosophy)   2. Epicurus.   3. Life.   4. Hydra (Greece)—
Description and travel.   I. Title.
B512.K54   2012
187—dc23   2012028559

Printed in the United States of America
1 3 5 7 9 10 8 6 4 2

Set in Adobe Garamond   •   *Designed by Elke Sigal*

For Eliana

It is not the young man who should be
considered fortunate but the old man who has
lived well, because the young man in his prime
wanders much by chance, vacillating in his
beliefs, while the old man has docked in the
harbor, having safeguarded his true happiness.

—EPICURUS

CONTENTS

Not what we have, but what we enjoy,
constitutes our abundance.

———————

—EPICURUS

Prologue

The Table at Dimitri's Taverna

....

ON SEEKING A PHILOSOPHY OF OLD AGE

....

He is sitting at a wooden table at the far rim of the terrace of Dimitri's taverna in the village of Kamini on the Greek island Hydra. Tucked behind his right ear is a sprig of wild lavender that, with considerable effort, he stooped to pick on his way here. From time to time—usually during lulls in conversation with his tablemates—he removes the herb, takes a few sniffs of it, and then returns it to its nesting spot. Leaning against the table to his right is an olive-wood cane topped with a pewter caryatid— a maiden of Karyai, the ancient Peloponnesian village where the temple was dedicated to the goddess Artemis. He takes this cane with him everywhere he goes, although he does not require it for walking: his gait is slow but steady. The cane is an emblem, a sign of his age. It is also a recognition of his life spent as a man; the ancient Greek word for "cane" refers to a rod that soldiers used for striking enemies. That his cane handle is a comely and shapely maiden may have some personal significance too; in his younger days he was known as a connoisseur of beautiful women.

I nod to him from my seat under the taverna's awning, where I have been reading a book titled *The Art of Happiness, or The Teachings of Epicurus.* He nods back with a slight tilt of his white-haired head, a tilt of dignified congeniality, and then returns to conversation with his friends. His name is Tasso and he is seventy-two years old. I have known him for many years now.

Although Tasso looks every year his age—his face and neck are covered with a fine crosshatch of deep lines—here he is still considered a handsome man, a handsome *old* man. He is said to "wear his age on his face," a compliment. When the French philosopher Albert Camus wrote in his novel *The Fall,* "Alas, after a certain age every man is responsible for his face," he too was voicing approval: a man's face tells the truth about him; the face a man acquires is the result of the choices he has made and the experiences that followed from those choices. The islanders say that on a man who has weathered challenging experiences, a finely seasoned face will emerge in old age. It is the face he has earned, and its raw beauty is in the fully lived life it expresses.

I eavesdrop on Tasso and his companions. As is their habit, they sit side by side and speak loudly to one another, so I have no difficulty hearing them. Although my Greek is rudimentary, I can catch the drift of their talk, a conversation that began before I arrived and will continue until the sun begins to drop behind the Peloponnese, just across the sea. It is aimless, cheerful chat, for the most part mundane. They talk about the sunlight, which is unusually hazy today, the new owner of a cheese stall in the port market, their children and grandchildren, the state of political affairs in Athens. Occasionally one tells a story from his past—usually one his companions have heard before. The talk is punctuated by leisurely, comfortable silences as they gaze out at the Peloponnesian straits.

—⚝—

I have returned to this Greek island on a personal quest: I am an old man myself now—seventy-three—and I want to figure out the most satisfying way to live this stage of my life. Having spent, over the years, several extended periods in Greece, I believe I may find some clues in the way old people live here. The old folks of Hydra have always struck me as uncommonly content with their stage in life.

I have also toted across the Atlantic a lean library of

philosophy books—most by ancient Greek thinkers, some by twentieth-century existentialists, plus an assortment of other favorites—because I think I may find some clues in these too. Since I was a college student, over fifty years ago, I have had an enduring interest in what the great philosophers have to say about how to live a valuable and gratifying life. I remember that some of these thinkers had intriguing ideas about how to live a fulfilling old age, although it was not a subject that particularly attracted me when I still had youthful ambitions (not to mention boundless energy and hair). The prospect of reading the ancient Greek philosophers while surrounded by the rocky, sunlit land-scape where their ideas first flourished feels just right to me.

～☡～

It was not a birthday epiphany or a shocking glimpse in the mir-ror that set the wheels of this personal journey turning; it was something far more prosaic—a visit to my dentist. After poking around in my mouth, Dr. Nacht earnestly informed me that due to normal, age-appropriate atrophy of my jawbone, a row of my lower teeth needed to be removed and replaced with implants. The only alternative, he said, would be a denture plate without any stable teeth to anchor it. With the denture, I would be sen-tenced to a diet devoid of steaks and pork chops, to frequent embarrassing incidents when my false teeth would pop loose and come out of my mouth attached to, say, a piece of toffee, and, worse yet, I would have the unmistakable clunky smile of an old man. I immediately signed up for the implants.

Back at home, I looked over my schedule for this procedure: a minimum of seven visits to the nearest oral surgeon, a good hour's drive away. These were spaced out over the course of almost a year. A quick look on the Web revealed that I could expect a few days of pain after each visit, not to mention an aggregate of several weeks during which I would basically subsist on baby food. And, of course, I would be out several thousand dollars. For what, again?

Pork chops? No embarrassing denture pop-outs? A more youthful smile?

I then realized just how much those potential denture pops and that old-mannish smile had figured in my instant decision to get the implants. But now those reasons did not make good sense to me. They did not seem to reflect my genuine values at this point in my life. In my early seventies did I really care if I presented to the world an old man's goofy smile? And even more to the point, with my years of clear thinking and reasonable mobility dwindling as quickly as my jawbone, did I honestly want to dedicate an entire year to regular visits to an oral surgeon?

I did not. And that was when I realized that, without thinking about it, I had been swept up in the current trend of trying to extend the prime of life well into the years that used to be called "old age." My unwitting participation in this trend went far beyond mere cosmetic issues to include the very way I perceived the amount of gratifying life left to me. I had been doing some fuzzy math. I had been caught up in an epidemic of denial. Without realizing it, I had routinely been opting for what I have come to think of as "youth implants."

This new old-age credo was everywhere I looked. If someone even casually mentioned that she was getting on in years, she was immediately chastened: "You're not old. You're still in your prime!" She was informed that "Seventy is the new fifty." She was admonished not to "give in" to old age.

This creed urges people my age to keep setting new goals, to charge ahead into new ventures, to design new programs for self-improvement. We are advised that medicine and its promise of an extended life span have given us an unprecedented opportunity: we can spin out the prime of our lives indefinitely. And if we surrender to old age, we are fools or, worse, cowards.

All around me, I saw many of my contemporaries remaining in their prime-of-life vocations, often working harder than ever. Others were setting off on expeditions to exotic destinations, copies of *1,000 Places to See Before You Die* tucked in their backpacks. Some were enrolling in classes in conversational French, taking up jogging, and even signing up for cosmetic surgery and youth-enhancing hormone treatments. A friend of mine in her late sixties had not only undergone a face-lift but also elected to have breast implants. And one man my age told me that between his testosterone patch and seventy-two-hour Cialis, he felt like a young buck again. "Forever Young" was my generation's theme song, and unreflectively I had been singing along with them.

It certainly is not hard to see the appeal of the "forever young" movement. The prime of my life has been, on balance, pretty satisfying, so why stop now? Why not more of a good thing? And more? And more?

But something about this new philosophy of old age does not sit right with me, and it took the prospect of those dental implants to prompt me to examine why. I suspect that if I were to take this popularly accepted route, I would miss out on something deeply significant: I would deny myself a unique and invaluable stage of life. I have deep-seated qualms about going directly from a protracted prime of life to *old* old age—the now attenuated period of senility and extreme infirmity that precedes death. I am seriously concerned that on that route I would miss for eternity ever simply being authentically and contentedly old.

The problem is that I am not entirely sure what an authentic old man is or how he should live. But I do have some hunches, and it is with them that I need to begin. At the very least, I believe an authentic old man would be honest with himself about how much fully conscious and rational life he has left. He would want to use that time in the best and most appropriate way. I

also suspect he might sense that this stage of life offers meaningful possibilities that were never before available to him.

But beyond that, I only have questions. And that is why I
have returned to this Greek island with a suitcase full of philosophy books.

—⚬—

One of Tasso's companions signals Dimitri to bring another
bottle of retsina and a few plates of mezes—some olives, stuffed
grape leaves, and a yogurt, cucumber, and garlic dip. They now
arrange themselves around the table so all are in reach of the
food. I have yet to see Dimitri present them with a bill, and I
believe he never does; the men will simply place a few coins on
the table when they leave—"old man" rates. Tasso pulls a deck
of cards from his pocket, and they begin to play *prefa*, their
preferred card game, with one of the four sitting out each hand
and taking up any slack in the conversation.

And I turn back to my book about Epicurus.

Chapter One

The Old Greek's Olive Trees

Epicurus grew up on another Aegean island, Samos, two hundred miles east of here, nearer to Anatolia, or Asia Minor. He was born in 341 BCE, only eighty years after Plato, but was little influenced by him. What Epicurus mainly had on his mind was the question of how to live the best possible life, especially considering that we only have one of them—Epicurus did not believe in an afterlife. This seems like the most fundamental philosophical question, the question of all questions. But students of the history of Western philosophy are often disheartened to find that as the centuries went on that question began to take a backseat to philosophical questions that were considered more pressing, like Martin Heidegger's mindblower that used to make me laugh out loud with incomprehension, "Why are there things that are rather than nothing?" and the epistemological problem, "How do we know what is real?" Epicurus certainly speculated about the nature of reality, but he did so fundamentally in service of his ultimate question, "How does one make the most of one's life?" Not a bad question.

Epicurus's answer, after many years of deep thought, was that the best possible life one could live is a happy one, a life filled with pleasure. At first look, this conclusion seems like a no-brainer, the sort of wisdom found on the side of a box of Celestial Seasonings tea. But Epicurus knew this was only a starting point because it raised the more troublesome and perplexing questions of what constitutes a happy life, which pleasures are truly gratifying and enduring, and which are fleeting and lead to pain, plus the monumental questions of why and how we often thwart ourselves from attaining happiness.

I have to admit that I experienced a pang of disillusionment when I first realized that Epicurus was not an epicurean, at least not in the way we currently use that term—that is, to mean a supreme sensualist with gourmet appetites. Let me put it this way: Epicurus preferred a bowl of plain boiled lentils to a plate of roasted pheasant infused with *mastiha* (a reduction painstakingly made from the sap of a nut tree), a delicacy slaves prepared for noblemen in ancient Greece. This was not the result of any democratic inclination but rather of Epicurus's hankering for personal comfort, which clearly included comfort foods. The pheasant dish titillated the taste buds, but Epicurus was not a sensualist in that sense: he was not looking for dazzling sensory excitement. No, bring on those boiled lentils! For one thing, he took great pleasure in food he had grown himself—that was part of the gratification of eating the lentils. For another, he had a Zen-like attitude about his senses: if he fully engaged in tasting the lentils, he would experience all the subtle delights of their flavor, delights that rival those of more extravagantly spiced fare. And another of this dish's virtues was that it was a snap to prepare. Epicurus was not into tedious, mindless work like, say, dripping *mastiha* onto a slow-roasting pheasant.

Some Athenians saw Epicurus and his ideas as a threat to social stability. A philosophy that set personal pleasure as life's highest goal and that openly advocated self-interest could dissolve the glue they believed held the republic together: *altruism*. Epicurus's brand of self-centeredness, they argued, did not make for good citizenship. But Epicurus and his followers could not have cared less what these detractors thought. For starters, Epicureans had little interest in the political process. Indeed they believed that to enjoy a truly gratifying life one should withdraw completely from the public sphere; society would function remarkably well if everyone simply adopted a live-and-let-live policy, with each man seeking his own happiness. This followed naturally from one of Epicurus's basic tenets: "It is impossible to live wisely and well and justly without living a pleasant life."

Epicurus was a man who lived his philosophy, and this entailed forming a protocommune, the Garden, on the outskirts of Athens, where he and a small and devoted group of friends lived simply, grew vegetables and fruit, ate together, and talked endlessly—mostly, of course, about Epicureanism. Anyone who wished to join them was welcome, as evidenced by the words inscribed on the Garden's gate: "Stranger, here you will do well to tarry; here our highest good is pleasure. The caretaker of that abode, a kindly host, will be ready for you; he will welcome you with bread, and serve you water also in abundance, with these words: 'Have you not been well entertained? This garden does not whet your appetite, but quenches it.'"

Not exactly a gourmet menu, but the price was right and the company intriguing.

Remarkably, contrary to the prevailing mores of Greece in Epicurus's era, women were well received in the Garden, where they were treated as equals in philosophical discussions. Even prostitutes were occasionally present at the table, feeding Athenian gossip that Epicurus and his followers were wanton hedonists. But this was clearly not the case: Epicureans much preferred tranquil pleasures to wild ones. The simple truth was that, unlike the other Hellenistic philosophies of that period, Epicureanism espoused and practiced a radical egalitarianism of both gender and social class.

Although most of Epicurus's original manuscripts have now been lost or destroyed (it is believed that he wrote over three hundred books, yet only three letters and a few sets of aphorisms survive intact), his philosophy spread throughout Greece in his own time and later took Italy by storm, particularly when the Roman poet Lucretius set down the basic Epicurean principles in his magnum opus, *The Nature of Things.* In no small part, the perpetuation of Epicurus's philosophy was due to his own fore-sight and pocketbook: in his last will he endowed a school to carry on his teachings.

ON OLD AGE AS THE PINNACLE OF LIFE

Epicurus believed that old age was the pinnacle of life, the best it gets. In the collection known as the "Vatican Sayings" (so named because the manuscript was discovered in the Vatican library in the nineteenth century), he is recorded as stating: "It is not the young man who should be considered fortunate but the old man who has lived well, because the young man in his prime wanders much by chance, vacillating in his beliefs, while the old man has docked in the harbor, having safeguarded his true happiness."

The idea of being an old man safe in the harbor buoys me up as I sit under Dimitri's awning, pondering the best way to spend this stage of my life. It is the notion of being free from vacillat-ing beliefs that gets to me. My understanding from Epicurus's other teachings is that he also is referring to the young man's vacillating *pursuits*, the ones that follow from his vacillating beliefs. Epicurus is pointing to what the Zen Buddhists call the emptiness of "striving," and in our culture striving is the hallmark of a man still in his prime.

The same goes for those of us who embrace the "forever young" credo: we don't give up setting ever new goals for ourselves, new ambitions to fulfill while we still can. Many forever youngsters are driven by the frustration of not having fully achieved the goals they dreamed of attaining when they were younger; they see their final years as a last chance to grab some elusive brass ring.

I became particularly aware of this phenomenon recently when the fiftieth-anniversary report of my college class arrived in the mail. One classmate, a highly successful lawyer and part-time theater and culture reporter for the *Wall Street Journal*, wrote: "Every day I think about what I haven't done and get anxious. That I remain in relatively good health is a great blessing, but it's also part of why I'm not sufficiently driven to finish the novels, plays, and nonfiction stewing in my head. . . . But there's time, I hope. We all hope, don't we?"

This man drew inspiration from Henry Wadsworth Longfellow's "Morituri Salutamus," the poem he wrote for the fiftieth anniversary of the class of 1825 of his alma mater, Bowdoin College. In the poem Longfellow urges his elderly classmates to keep busy, *very* busy.

> *Ah, nothing is too late*
> *Till the tired heart shall cease to palpitate.*
> *Cato learned Greek at eighty; Sophocles*
> *Wrote his grand Oedipus, and Simonides*
> *Bore off the prize of verse from his compeers,*
> *When each had numbered more than fourscore years,*
> *And Theophrastus, at fourscore and ten,*
> *Had but begun his "Characters of Men."*

That "nothing is too late" refrain certainly is tempting. We septuagenarians just might be at the top of our game, our creative juices overflowing. Would Epicurus have us dam them up? Would he have sacrificed the classical masterpiece *Oedipus Rex* just so Sophocles could sit happily in the harbor? That sounds like a terrible waste.

Still, there is no rest for the striver. Just beyond the completion of each goal on our life-achievement "bucket list" looms another goal, and then another. Meanwhile, of course, the clock is ticking—quite loudly, in fact. We become breathless. And we have no time left for a calm and reflective appreciation of our twilight years, no deliciously long afternoons sitting with friends or listening to music or musing about the story of our lives. And we will never get another chance for that.

It is not an easy decision.

ON FREEING OURSELVES FROM
THE PRISON OF EVERYDAY AFFAIRS

For me, it is Epicurus's overall assessment of the qualities of a truly satisfying life that sheds the brightest sunshine on what a good old age might be. High on his list of the ways we thwart happiness is by binding ourselves to the constraints of the "commercial world." Epicurus may have predated Madison Avenue by a few millennia, but he already detected the commercial world's uncanny ability to make us think we need stuff we don't—and, as the world of commerce keeps chugging along, to need ever *newer* stuff. But when shopping for the latest thing—usually something we do not really need—Epicurus's all-important life of tranquil pleasure is nowhere to be found. One of my favorite of Epicurus's aphorisms is: "Nothing is enough for the man to whom enough is too little."

In Epicurus's view, true happiness is a bargain, like, say, boiled lentils—or a yogurt dip. In a serene old age, who really feels deprived if he can't feast on slow-roasted pheasant or, for that matter, the poached salmon with truffles my wife and I dined on just before my departure for Greece? Go with the simple pleasures, Epicurus says. They are not only less expensive, they are less taxing on an old body.

Yet when Epicurus writes, "We must free ourselves from the prison of everyday affairs and politics," he has more on his mind than just freeing ourselves from the endless acquisition of unnecessary stuff. It is the business of dedicating our lives to business that he is warning us against, starting with the obvious restraints of having a boss who tells us what to do, how to do it, and what is wrong with the way we are currently doing it. Even if one *is* the boss, as many of my "forever young" friends are, one's freedom remains constrained by the politics of having to deal with other people; one still has to tell *them* what to do, to negotiate with and motivate them. One is still imprisoned. And freedom—Epicurus's brand of radical existential freedom—is absolutely necessary for a happy life.

Forsaking the world of commerce—that is, giving up one's day job—may have been all well and good in the Garden in 380 BCE (and I do have to wonder if a frequent guest at Epicurus's table, the financier Idomeneus, didn't pitch in to purchase the goods that couldn't be grown in their communal vegetable patch, like the barrels of wine they were said to have consumed daily), but it feels like a tougher choice nowadays. In today's terms, Epicurus would advocate a kind of sixties, getting-by-on-nothing lifestyle—one that, for better or for worse, few of us were willing to fully embrace to attain perfect freedom when we were younger.

Heaven knows, I tried. Back in the late sixties when the mantra of my former professor Timothy Leary, "Turn on, tune in, drop out," reverberated in the zeitgeist, I quit my job writing for television shows in New York and came for the first time to this very place, Hydra. Living on money I had saved, I did nothing for an entire year but sit in tavernas with locals and other dropouts, drink ouzo, chase after women, and stare off into the middle distance.

One morning, during this idyll, I was idling in the port when, astonishingly, a Harvard classmate suddenly appeared in front of me; he had just stepped off a yacht on a vacation cruise. I was deeply tanned, I had not had a haircut since my arrival on the island half a year earlier, and I was wearing well-worn clothes. The classmate was startled to find me in this place and in that condition and wanted to know what the hell I was doing here. "I'm taking my retirement early while I can still enjoy it," I replied. It was meant to be wit but belied more defensiveness than I had realized I felt.

That long-ago year on Hydra was supremely enjoyable—I have no regrets about it—but truth to tell, I gradually became bored with myself. I yearned to get busy. I wanted to be engaged in the world. I wanted to make something of myself. And so I returned to the world of commerce, although my attraction to the Epicurean life never completely left me.

Now, sitting at Dimitri's, I see that it is Tasso's turn to skip a hand of *prefa*. He stands, cane in hand, and ambles to the seaward edge of the terrace, where he watches the ferry from Ermioni appear from behind Dokos, a stark, uninhabited, whale-shaped island that lies between here and the Peloponnese. This ferry is one of the last of the slow-moving vessels sailing here; for decades now the most popular boat has been a hydrofoil from Piraeus—a hermetic sardine can of a conveyance for getting hurriedly to a place where time slows to a standstill.

The creeping ferry from Ermioni reminds me of the two trains that circumnavigate the Peloponnese, one in each direction; these also move at a pace not much faster than a middle-aged jogger. At times these trains rattle on so leisurely that one could easily pick oranges from trackside trees through the windows. No doubt this speaks to the not-up-to-snuffness of rural Greek technology, but it also speaks wonderfully to the Greek predilection for focusing on the pleasures of the journey, rather than on the destination.

On one of my many returns to Greece, I rode these trains around the perimeter of the Peloponnese, with my wife and daughter. It was the year 2000, and Greece, after failing to qualify for entry into the euro as currency in 1999, was trying again. My wife, who is from Holland, surveyed the scene outside our window with a sardonic eye, spotting "inefficiencies" everywhere. "Look at them!" she would howl as we passed a group of five Greeks leisurely unloading a cartload of eggplants bucket-brigade style, several with cigarettes dangling from their lips. "These people aren't serious about the euro!" Although she was smiling, she was at least half-serious; Holland, of course, is the

world capital of Calvinism. My daughter and I soon assigned
her the nickname "the euro inspector."

One morning, after a magical few days in the northern Peloponnesian village of Diakofto, we made our way to the railway
station to catch the train to Corinth. My grade-school-level
Greek qualified me as our tour leader; I bought the tickets and
found us seats on the departing train, where I immediately
spread out my limbs and drifted into a pleasant snooze. Minutes
later I was awakened by my wife—we were going in the wrong
direction! We had gotten on the train circling the Peloponnesian
peninsula counterclockwise instead of the one circling it clock-
wise. My wife realized this when our train passed a bench hold-
ing the same three old men we had passed when we'd come from
the other direction a few days before. "It's as if they never
moved," she said. My whimsical daughter chimed in that we
must be on a time-traveling train and were rolling back into the
past. *Indeed*.

Clearly it was my responsibility to rectify the situation. I
found the conductor seated at the front of our car, where he was
drinking coffee from an espresso-size ceramic cup—I learned
later that when he wanted more coffee he simply exchanged this
cup for a full one proffered through the window by waiters from
various railway station cafés along the way. I wished the conductor a good morning, and he immediately urged me to sit down
across from him, begging my pardon for not being able to offer

me some coffee. I told him about my train mix-up. He laughed and said in English, "It happens all the time. You only had a fifty-fifty chance of getting on the right one."

But for the next few minutes that subject had to wait for more significant matters: Was I from New York? Possibly Queens? Astoria? Oh, from Massachusetts? Did I know the Manikis family in Boston? They came from the same village as his wife. During this genial schmooze, I kept my eyes averted from my wife's urgent stare. After the conductor and I finally came to a satisfactory resolution of our round of Greek American demography—I *did* know George Genaris in Lenox, Massachusetts, whose grandfather hailed from Patras—the conductor picked up a radiotelephone the size of a wooden shoe, pressed some buttons, and spoke a few words in rapid dialect that I suspect would have been as unintelligible to a native Athenian as it was to me. Smiling, he then instructed me to get my family and luggage prepared to disembark. We did as told.

Several minutes later, our train came to a gentle stop beside an apricot grove. We now saw that the train coming from the opposite direction had also stopped here. The passengers from that train had stepped outside and were lounging among the apricot trees. Someone among them had produced a jug of a yogurt drink that was being passed around, some were smoking cigarettes, a few had picked ripe apricots and were munching on them, and all were chatting amiably. Our conductor saluted his counterpart, gestured toward us, and bade us a warm farewell.

And then we realized what had just happened: hearing of our plight, the engineer of the oncoming train had brought it to a halt, and his passengers, apparently without complaint—indeed seeming to take pleasure in this unexpected intermission—had disembarked to wait for us. Personal schedules, if there had been any, evaporated. This train was definitely not going to be running on time. Talk about inefficiency! This would never happen in Holland.

My daughter and I turned to the "euro inspector" and laughed so hard we could barely walk across the tracks.

Recalling this episode now, I am convinced I have come to the right part of the world to meditate on the best way to live my old age.

EPICUREANISM AS A LIVING
PHILOSOPHY TODAY

Unsurprisingly, Epicurus's laid-back legacy survives more thoroughly in Greece's rural areas than in its cities. Aegean islanders like to tell a joke about a prosperous Greek American who visits one of the islands on vacation. Out on a walk, the affluent Greek American comes upon an old Greek man sitting on a rock, sipping a glass of ouzo, and lazily staring at the sun setting into the sea. The American notices there are olive trees growing on the hills behind the old Greek but that they are untended, with olives just dropping here and there onto the ground. He asks the old man who the trees belong to.

"They're mine," the Greek replies.

"Don't you gather the olives?" the American asks.

"I just pick one when I want one," the old man says.

"But don't you realize that if you pruned the trees and picked the olives at their peak, you could sell them? In America everybody is crazy about virgin olive oil, and they pay a damned good price for it."

"What would I do with the money?" the old Greek asks.

"Why, you could build yourself a big house and hire servants to do everything for you."

"And then what would I do?"

"You could do anything you want!"

"You mean, like sit outside and sip ouzo at sunset?"

ON THE TRICKLE-DOWN EFFECT
OF PHILOSOPHICAL IDEAS

Would it be naive to imagine that a philosopher from the third century BCE inspired a random group of contemporary Greeks to uncomplainingly accept—even enjoy—an unscheduled interlude in an apricot grove? I don't think so.

To begin with, back in Epicurus's time, and the periods immediately before and after it, the ideas of philosophers, poets, and playwrights reached far beyond the Garden's dining table or the steps of the Acropolis or the Theater of Dionysus and into ordinary Athenians' everyday conversations. By all accounts, this was a civilization that liked to talk and made the time to do so. Later forms of communication, like the frequently one-way media of our era, did not yet offer competition to daily dialogue. Attending a performance at the Dionysus amphitheater was often an all-day affair in which the audience was cast in the role of a jury that deliberated on which character's actions and viewpoint was most worthy. After-theater discussions about justice, proper conduct, and human frailties could get hot and heady. These people were talking about *ideas*.

The Athenian populace also talked about philosophers' ideas. And because Epicurus welcomed men and women of all social classes—even slaves—at his ongoing symposia, his ideas flowed freely into the general public. This flow was undoubtedly assisted by the fact that, like all talky societies, ancient Athens thrived on gossip; the Athenians even had a goddess of rumor and gossip, Ossa. Epicurus's garden, what with its prostitutes and washerwomen at the table, was often a subject of general gossip, and whatever its indignities, gossip can be a powerful vehicle for new and interesting ideas.

Epicurus's ideas about the best way to live resonated for many Athenians. These ideas offered them new ways to see themselves and their personal options: "Hmm, if that fellow Epicurus is right, and the ultimate purpose of life is to maximize life's pleasures and not, say, to earn enough money to commission a statue of myself so I will be immortalized in marble, then maybe I should cut back on my job painting maidens on vases and spend more time just hanging out and appreciating life." All right, maybe I got a little carried away with my vase-painter fantasy, but something very much like it appears to have happened all around old Athens.

Of course, this does not tell us if Epicurus's philosophy has actually *endured* in Greek culture over the millennia. The relatively new discipline of sociobiology would argue that Greek DNA is the root cause for the sunniness of those Peloponnesians unexpectedly and happily detained in that apricot grove. Expanding on Darwinian theory, sociobiology contends that, in addition to physical characteristics, psychological and social characteristics evolve through natural selection in a particular geographical environment and climate. A frequently cited example of how sociobiology functions in the animal kingdom is the "altruism" practiced by specific members of various species, including the leaf-cutter ant and the vampire bat. These particular members behave in ways that benefit others in their extended families while not directly benefiting the individuals who make the generous sacrifices themselves. In the end, the entire species is better able to survive as a result of this behavior; thus the "altruistic" genes get passed down through the generations. Furthermore, similar species that do not have altruistic members sometimes die out because of their absence.

A sociobiologist, then, might hypothesize that in Greece's rocky terrain, and under its hot sun, early Greeks who became extremely anxious due to an unanticipated turn of events were more likely to die from stress-related illnesses before they could reproduce than more carefree Greeks; therefore the more carefree, stress-resistant Greeks—and their DNA—were naturally selected. I suppose that hypothesis is within the realm of possibility. In any event, sociobiologists basically would say it is more likely that those Peloponnesian travelers happily accepted their unexpected interlude in that apricot grove as a result of genetics than because of some philosophical tradition that was handed down to them through hundreds of generations.

But perhaps both explanations are true: maybe a disposition toward a carefree outlook and day-to-day gratefulness naturally evolved in Greek DNA *and* Epicurus analyzed that natural disposition and rendered it in discrete and coherent ideas. Ultimately, his ideas became a living, conscious philosophy of life that has endured through the ages along with the Greeks' naturally evolved predispositions. And one thing about a conscious philosophy is that it allows people to *consciously* deliberate about their options: "I suppose I could complain to the engineer that this unscheduled stop in the apricot grove will make me late for dinner, but wouldn't it better reflect my true values if I simply enjoyed to the fullest this surprising little respite?"

This, in the end, is the prime purpose of a philosophy: to

give us lucid ways to think about the world and how to live in it. That is what I am up to, sitting here with my book on Epicurean philosophy in front of me: deliberating about my options for a good old age. There is nothing I can do about my DNA, but perhaps Epicurus and other philosophers can help me sort out the choices I need to make.

ON CHOOSING AN EPICUREAN
LIFE IN OLD AGE

Opting for Epicurean freedom in old age makes terrific sense to me. The timing is perfect because this kind of freedom is available to many of us past the age of sixty-five without our having to pitch a lean-to in the woods or take up residence in a commune—although, come to think of it, living on a commune as an old man might be just the ticket. In any event, Epicurean freedom in old age might be an excellent choice for people debating the "forever young" option; by and large we are people with retirement resources, even if those funds may be insufficient for gourmet meals or even, possibly, for the homes in which we have lived during our productive years. Epicurus would have us scale down and taste the sweetness of this freedom.

Freed from "the prison of everyday affairs and politics," an old man needs only to answer to himself. He does not need to stick to a strict schedule or compromise his whims to sustain his life. He can, for example, sit for hours on end in the company of his friends, occasionally pausing to sniff the fragrance of a sprig of wild lavender.

ON THE PLEASURES OF
COMPANIONSHIP IN OLD AGE

Perhaps without fully realizing it, a good portion of the pleasure Tasso finds at his table at Dimitri's is that he is enjoying his companions *without wanting anything from them.* His tablemates are a retired fisherman, a retired teacher, and a retired waiter—all born and raised on the island—while Tasso is a former Athenian judge, who as a young man studied law in Thessaloníki and London. But this has little, if any, bearing on his relationship with his three friends.

Wanting nothing from one's friends is fundamentally different from the orientation of a person who is still immersed in professional life and its relationships. An individual in commerce, whatever that commerce may be, is in service of a goal that has little or nothing to do with genuine friendship. A boss gives instructions because she wants results, and an employee follows her instructions for the same reason, one of those desired results being his paycheck. No matter how many management manuals propose treating employees and colleagues as genuine individuals, the underlying fact remains that a commercial situation is always inherently political. On the job, our colleagues are first and foremost means to an end, and so are we. So it always was. Epicurus understood this when he cautioned us about the perils of commerce and politics.

In Kantian ethics, we are specifically advised never to treat another human being as a means but always as an end in himself. In his monumental *Groundwork for the Metaphysics of Morals,* Immanuel Kant concluded that an abstract and absolute principle for all ethical behavior was required as the touchstone for all particular moral choices. The principle he deduced was his Golden Rule–like supreme categorical imperative: "Act only according to that maxim whereby you can, at the same time, will that it should become a universal law." Thus Kant believed that in following this imperative no man would choose to treat another man as a means to an end; he could not rationally will that such behavior become universal law, in large part because then he too would be treated as a means by others.

Treating someone as an end rather than as a means turns out to be as much a treat for us as for the person to whom we are relating. Tasso does not want anything from his friend the fisherman except his company. He does not want him to tighten up his summary of a case before the court, as he frequently desired a lawyer to do during his days on the bench. Tasso feels no need to manipulate, exploit, or in any way maneuver his fisherman-companion to do anything. No, Tasso simply wants his friend to *be* with him. He wants him to share conversation, laughter, a hand of *prefa*, and, perhaps most important, to share the silence when they both gaze out at the sea. Epicureans consider communal silence a hallmark of true friendship.

For an old man with the world of "everyday affairs and politics" behind him, this kind of camaraderie is the greatest gift. It is a gift that rarely, if ever, is fully available to the forever youngsters still immersed in their careers.

—⁓—

Companionship was at the top of Epicurus's list of life's pleasures. He wrote, "Of all the things that wisdom provides to help one live one's entire life in happiness, the greatest by far is the possession of friendship."

It may come as a shock to the well-heeled members of the New England Epicurean Society, an exclusive dining club that favors caviar and oysters at its black-tie dinners, but Epicurus believed that choosing with whom one eats dinner is far more significant than choosing what the menu should be. "Before you eat or drink anything, carefully consider with whom you eat or drink rather than what you eat or drink, because eating without a friend is the life of the lion or the wolf."

By the joys of friendship, Epicurus meant a full range of human interactions ranging from intimate and often philosophical discussions with his dearest companions—the kind he enjoyed at the long dining table in the Garden—to impromptu exchanges with people, known and unknown, in the street. The education or social status of those with whom he conversed mattered not a whit; in fact the height of true friendship was to be accepted and loved for who one was, not what station in life one had achieved. Loving and being loved affirmed one's sense of self and conquered feelings of loneliness and alienation. It kept one sane.

If this prescription for happiness sounds like the drivel of popular songs (in my youth, Nat King Cole's hit-parade rendition of "Nature Boy" concluded, "The greatest thing you'll ever learn is just to love and be loved in return"), so be it. It may still happen to be true. The philosopher from Samos was certainly convinced it was true. And there is no doubting friendship's unique availability in the years when politics and commerce are behind us.

My lifelong friend and frequent cowriter, Tom Cathcart, and I have always gotten a big kick out of striking up conversations with strangers we meet on trains and planes, in bookstores, on neighboring park benches. Tom has a particular talent for drawing personal stories from these people, and we both love hearing them. But far more valuable to us than the entertainment of the stories is the connection made with another human being. It is a comfort like no other. It is the comfort of personal communion.

Now that Tom and I are old men and look it—we are both balding, with gray beards—we find that making these impromptu connections happens more easily. It took us a while to figure out why this was so, and when we did, we had a good laugh: old guys are unthreatening. We don't look like we are up to no good, for the simple reason that we don't look like we are *capable* of inflicting any no-goodness—well, other than being seriously boring. It was a bittersweet moment when we realized that none of the women with whom we initiated conversations suspected for a minute that we were coming on to them. Heartbreaking to admit, but they were right.

ON THE COMFORT OF
COMMISERATION IN OLD AGE

At Tasso's table, the retired teacher has asked to skip the next hand of cards. He needs to pee, the third time in the past hour. It's his damned prostate gland, he moans. His companions tease him. The fisherman says his friend's prostate is so big he could use it for bait to catch a shark. The teacher stalks off to the WC, grumbling, and I am reminded of Montaigne's recommendation to vigorously gripe about illnesses.

Michel de Montaigne, the sixteenth-century French essayist, was well acquainted with Epicurus's ideas. Recapping the Greek philosopher's pleasure calculus, he wrote, "And with Epicurus, I conceive that pleasures are to be avoided if greater pains be the consequence, and pains to be coveted that will terminate in greater pleasures." Like Epicurus, Montaigne was convinced that friendship, and the good conversation that comes with it, was the greatest pleasure available to us. In his essay "Of Vanity," the French philosopher wrote: "I know that the arms of friendship are long enough to reach from the one end of the world to the other."

Montaigne wrote at length about old age and, in one piece, he suggests that complaining to friends about the infirmities of old age is the best medicine: "If the body find itself relieved by complaining, let it complain; if agitation ease it, let it tumble and toss at pleasure; if it seem to find the disease evaporate (as some physicians hold that it helps women in delivery) in making loud outcries, or if this do but divert its torments, let it roar as it will."

Thus Montaigne insists that if we don't let it all hang out in front of our friends, we are cheating ourselves out of one of an old person's best palliatives—all in the name of some kind of dumb propriety. These days, in some circles of old folks, this recapitulation of complaints is known as "the organ recital," and, God knows, it does "divert [the] torments," at least for a bit.

ON FACING DEATH BLISSFULLY

The sun has begun its descent, appearing to enlarge as it nears the horizon and to dim as its rays gradually become eclipsed by our planet. Its refracted beams cast a pale, rose-colored glow onto the water, and all four men at Tasso's table suspend their conversation to watch daylight's finale.

Epicurus was not afraid of death. He famously said, "Death is nothing to us, since when we are, death has not come, and when death has come, we are not. The absence of life is not evil; death is no more alarming than the nothingness before birth."

Later philosophers, especially Søren Kierkegaard, the Danish philosopher and theologian, took exception to Epicurus's dictum, finding it simplistic. After all "when we are" we are still *conscious* of the fact that in the future we will no longer be, and that makes one hell of a difference. In fact, according to Kierkegaard, it is enough to strike a man, young or old, with "fear and trembling."

Although all the men at Tasso's table are at least nominally Greek Orthodox Christians, a religion that promises a beatific afterlife to the godly, my guess is that, like most mortals, they are not entirely immune to this terror. Nonetheless they would recognize the comfort in Epicurus's dying words to his friend Idomeneus: "On this blissful day, which is also the last of my life, I write this to you. My continual sufferings from strangury [bladder spasms] and dysentery are so great that nothing could increase them; but I set above them all the gladness of mind at the memory of our past conversations."

In every real man a child is hidden
who wants to play.

———

—FRIEDRICH NIETZSCHE

Chapter Two

The Deserted Terrace

....

ON TIME AND WORRY BEADS

....

Seen from the sea, Hydra seems as flimsy as a hallucination. A lucent mist envelopes the island, and the incoming hydrofoil throws up a spray that further filters its landscape, softens it, makes it appear to float. But here on the island, even when the sky is as cloudy as it is today, every view is severe with detail. The shadow of a rock a mile off on the Peloponnesian shore appears as well defined as the lemon tree just outside my window. And because Hydra rises from its main port in a steep, horseshoe-shaped hill that is girded with houses, everyone is an innocent spectator to private scenes in remote courtyards and terraces.

At this moment I spy a middle-aged woman in a floral-patterned housecoat hanging out her laundry while carrying on a lively conversation with a brown-and-white cat perched on her garden wall; two terraces above her, I see a pair of grade school children sitting cross-legged under their garden door's awning, one pulling a picture book from his backpack, the other biting into a chunk of bread slathered with honey; and at the top of the hill, I can clearly make out a tall and portly Orthodox priest in black robe and chimney-pot hat sitting stoically on his garden bench while his diminutive wife, standing just behind him, lectures him, possibly about some item he failed to purchase on his morning trip to the port.

This is the celebrated trick of Hydra light: it transforms daily life into intimate theater.

In the whitewashed nineteenth-century house where I am staying, all the windows are screened with two crossed iron bars. "To keep the Turks out," some islanders say. "To keep Albanian pirates out," say others. Clearly these iron bars work: neither Turk nor Albanian has clambered into my room. The bars do not obscure the view from my desk window; rather they frame it into four discrete images: a hill studded with houses in one frame, a grove of almond trees in another, the harbor, the sea.

My lodging is high on the hill. Through the harbor frame, I now view the terrace of Dimitri's taverna, and it is empty. The clouds threaten rain, so I imagine that Tasso and his tablemates are either inside the café or skipping today's symposium.

But rain or not, I am hungry. As the figs in the hanging mesh basket in my room are in that awkward stage between fresh and dried, I set off for Dimitri's taverna, passing Tasso's house along the way. I catch a glimpse of him, sitting alone on his third-story terrace, where he appears deep in thought.

—⁓—

The only people inside Dimitri's are Dimitri himself, sitting in the kitchen and listening to the BBC World Service news and, at the far end of the dining area, by the window, his eighty-year-old father, Ianos, who is reading yesterday's Athenian newspaper while playing with his *kombolói*, a loop of thirty-three amber beads that are known in English as worry beads.

Like many of the island's men, Dimitri was a sailor when he was younger. He worked his way up to ship's radio operator, a job at which he picked up fluent English and a smattering of other languages, both Western and Eastern. When he reached his midthirties, he returned permanently to Hydra, opened his taverna, and married the local woman he had hired as his cook. The idea that life has natural, discrete stages comes intuitively to Dimitri.

I realize I have seen far fewer men fingering worry beads than when I first came to the island in the 1960s, and I ask Dimitri if that tradition is fading. Before responding, he signals for me to select my meal from the open metal trays at the front of the kitchen. As always I have a choice between moussaka, stuffed zucchinis, pastitsio (a Greek macaroni and cheese, with ground meat, which got its name from the Italian *pasticcio*, meaning "hodgepodge," a term that could describe most Greek dishes), and Dimitri's pièce de résistance, roasted lamb with potatoes. I spring for the lamb, despite the fact that a small party of flies is cavorting in its gravy. Dimitri turns off the radio, serves me up a generous platter of the lamb, pours two glasses of retsina, and sits down across from me.

"To start with, 'worry beads' is an ignorant translation," he begins. "It says more about the way English people think than it does about the Greeks. *Kombolói* have nothing to do with worrying."

Whenever Dimitri and I have these conversations, he assumes a teacherly air with more than a hint of strained patience, but nonetheless it is clear to me that he enjoys his role as my cultural interpreter. He is, in fact, an unusually astute and cosmopolitan man.

"*Kombolói* have to do with time, with spacing it out, making it last," he goes on.

Spacing time out? Making it last? Like many Greeks I know, Dimitri slips naturally into metaphysical pronouncements, although he certainly would not call them that. Dimitri is simply expressing his worldview, and that worldview sees time as a malleable thing, multidimensional, based not just on planetary movements and clocks but also on the way we personally appre-

vehicle, so there are no fragmentary scenes of faces and objects that remain perpetually unfinished, no mosaics forever missing critical tiles.

Because the island is a string of mountains and the terrain is rocky down to the shore, the pathways are mostly steps up and down, making walking relatively slow, both to avoid stumbling and to conserve energy. And because these paths twist sharply around boulders and houses, the passing view is divided into complete and comprehensible scenes. In only a matter of a few calendar days here, my internal clock adopts this tempo, and along with that comes a slowed-down appreciation of just about everything—of what I hear and see around me and of the feeling of the movements of my body.

Old people move slowly. Our rocky terrain is internal — fragile bones, faltering muscles, weakened hearts. As our slowness is a result of these failings, it is often viewed as a failing too—our feebleness on slow-motion display.

But simply because we old folks are forced into slower movements—as, for different reasons, Hydriots are—does that mean it is not a good thing? Being in this place where my old man's gait is matched step-by-step all around me, I now realize that I habitually fight against a leisurely pace; I resist giving in to slowness. This has been yet another of my unconscious conformities to the "forever young" ethos. Yet now it seems quite clear to me that slowness has extraordinary virtues.

Moving slowly has a grace to it that I find I can easily settle into. I feel fluent in slow motion. There is even something aesthetic about it, a flowing quality reminiscent of a tai chi sequence yet without that exercise's strict discipline. At times, climbing unhurriedly out of my chair, first testing my balance, then rising carefully to my feet and walking in measured steps to the window, I feel like I am performing an old man's natural, graceful dance. Impulse and movement match. Yes, I am giving in to a limitation of old age, but it does not feel like a defeat at all. In fact, sometimes it feels downright dignified.

Epicurus would have us savor each moment of our lives to the maximum, and fully savoring our experiences requires time. Sure, one reason I chew this chunk of Dimitri's lamb slowly is because of my erratic dentures. But this slow chewing also adds to my delight in this morsel; slowness is its relish.

In her essay on time, Hoffman contrasts slow "lived time" with her first experience of American time when she immigrated to the United States: "It was not only that time moved faster in America—it pressed onwards in more stressful ways." She observed American time's relationship to American anxiety: "Everyone suffered from the stress of not doing enough, or the possibility of doing more, or at least feeling good or guilty about it."

It is this time pressing onward that the forever young often choose as their "lived time," the tempo they set for the final stage of their lives. Indeed, from this viewpoint lived time may press onward with particular urgency, the urgency that comes from the knowledge that we are running out of time; we experience a kind of panicky *kairós*.

ON BOREDOM IN OLD AGE

The forever young have a compelling reason for opting for hurried time: it is their primary strategy for combating time's chronic tormentor—boredom. And next to illness and death, boredom is what we fear most in old age.

Nothing appears quite so potentially boring as being an old man without any new goals or upcoming exciting experiences, an old man without the buzz of a hungry libido, an old man whose energy level is gradually sinking to the point where the prospect of camping out in the woods seems more like an ordeal than recreation. And added to this is the fact that inevitably— the gatherings on Dimitri's terrace notwithstanding—an old man finds himself alone more often than ever before in his life. Lots of time, nothing to do. The blankness of boredom.

Another book I packed for this trip was *A Philosophy of Boredom*, by the Norwegian philosopher Lars Svendsen, and it was well worth the space it took up in my baggage. It is that rare book of contemporary philosophy that combines keen scholarship with a sympathetic concern for the stuff we ordinary humans worry about.

Svendsen points out that boredom is a relatively new idea

that arose out of late-eighteenth-century romanticism and its emphasis on the primacy of the individual. Instead of contentedly accepting their role in society and its traditions, people were urged by the romantic ideal to create their individual identity and, along with that, their own meaning of life. The drawback, writes Svendsen, is that "a society that functions well promotes man's ability to find meaning in the world; one that functions badly does not. In premodern societies there is usually a collective meaning that is sufficient. For us 'Romantics,' things are more problematic." Meaning does not come easily, or even at all, to many of us, especially to those of us who have lost a secure connection to a traditional God and religion.

In "existential boredom," as compared to "situational boredom" (for example, the feeling that overcomes me while sitting for two hours in the waiting room of my urologist), a person is locked inside a self that cannot find meaning in anything at all, a self that often has given up even trying to find meaning in anything. It is that feeling of pervasive emptiness best captured by the French word *ennui*, a word that gained popularity in English via Cole Porter's song "I Get a Kick Out of You":

> *But practically everything leaves me totally cold.*
> *The only exception I know is the case*
> *Where I'm out on a quiet spree*
> *Fighting vainly the old ennui. . . .*

With nothing meaningful in life, nothing is interesting. Enter boredom. A bored man even longs for longing. He has time to fill, but there is nothing compelling to do. He is bored to death. Those of us prone to melancholy are all too familiar with the feeling of existential boredom.

So, according to Svendsen, in order to fill his time, modern man got busy cooking up personal goals, seeking out challenging activities, and, most significantly, looking for *newness*. New experiences and new things couldn't possibly be boring, could they? Well, apparently they often could. After finally getting to be vice president of the company, another goal looms just ahead—becoming senior vice president, then president, then president of a larger company, and then of an even larger one. It can feel endless and never completely satisfying, and at a certain point it can start to feel pointless. Newness itself gets old. At the twelfth place to see before dying, viewing exotic terrain can get to be old hat—you've already done "exotic" eleven times. Old people are often particularly conscious of the half-life of newness. The phrases "the more things change, the more they remain the same" and "nothing would surprise me at this point in my life" come easily to our lips.

If a man cannot invest his life, or any part of it, with meaning, all he has left are distractions from meaninglessness, although few of us acknowledge them as such. But here and there we probably have intimations that these distractions are meaningless themselves. Svendsen writes, "The most hyperactive of us are precisely those who have the lowest boredom thresholds. We have an almost complete lack of downtime, scurrying from one activity to the next because we cannot face tackling time that is 'empty.' Paradoxically enough, this bulging time is often frighteningly empty when viewed in retrospect."

I can relate, especially in my old age. Looking back at the entire year I spent desperately trying to capture the heart of a certain wild, glamorous, and extremely fickle woman, I now see quite clearly that I had convinced myself that winning her would give my life some desperately needed meaning. At the time, I was recently back from my dropout year and having one hell of a time trying to reignite the enthusiasm I once had for writing funny stuff for television. I felt lost—at loose ends. Of course, chasing this woman ultimately did not give my life any meaning; in fact at a certain point, after breathlessly achieving my goal, I became bored. I inevitably returned to the emptiness that had sent me running after her in the first place.

The predestined disappointment built into desperately yearned-for newness has found its expression in many ironic aphorisms, like the bedouin saying, "Beware of what you desire, for you shall always get it." And my favorite, from Oscar Wilde: "In this world there are only two tragedies. One is not getting what one wants, and the other is getting it. The last is much the worst."

In Svendsen's view, modern man has tried to deal with boredom by treating the symptoms instead of the disease, by searching for "meaning surrogates"—like my fickle woman—instead of sitting still and, just possibly, contemplating what a meaningful life might be.

The "forever young" strategy of combating old age's boredom with super busyness certainly sounds like the "same old, same old"—an epilogue of "meaning surrogates" right up until the bitter end.

But what's an old man to do if he doesn't keep busy? Vegetate? Sleep all day? Relentlessly bellyache, as my mother did, about the fact that she, *of all people*, had been singled out to become an old lady?

ON PLAYING IN OLD AGE

For many philosophers, idleness—both the idleness that is forced upon us and the idleness we choose—is actually one of old age's greatest gifts. It gives us time for that wondrous human activity, *play*. In his popular political essay "In Praise of Idleness," the twentieth-century British philosopher Bertrand Russell chides us for failing to use our free time for, of all things, *fun*: "It will be said that, while a little leisure is pleasant, men would not know how to fill their days if they had only four hours of work out of the twenty-four. In so far as this is true in the modern world, it is a condemnation of our civilization; it would not have been true at any earlier period. There was formerly a capacity for light-heartedness and play which has been to some extent inhibited by the cult of efficiency. The modern man thinks that everything ought to be done for the sake of something else, and never for its own sake."

The contemporary wit Steven Wright makes a comparable point more succinctly: "Hard work pays off in the future. Laziness pays off now."

Play's the thing wherein we old folks can be rescued from boredom; that is, if we can only remember *how* to play. Russell got it right: just having fun for its own sake has been devalued to a waste of time, and as a result we seem to have lost our capacity for one of life's greatest delights, a delight to which we old folk are singularly suited.

Another book I brought with me is the classic text on recreation *Homo Ludens: A Study of the Play Element in Culture*, by the Dutch historian and philosopher Johan Huizinga. Alas, unlike Svendsen, who brings boredom to life, Huizinga analyzes play to death; after several dozen philological deconstructions of the words "seriousness" and "fun," we really do get the idea that the two concepts have very little in common. Still, some of Huizinga's ideas strike me as pertinent to a philosophy of old age.

Not only is play a human cultural universal, but most animals are top-notch players too. Whether it is a pair of bear cubs splashing one another in a stream (where, judging by their mother's impatient reaction, they are *supposed* to be learning how to fish) or my dog, Snookers, running ever-expanding circles around the spruce tree in our yard back home—the animal instinct for aimless fun is clearly built in. Ditto for us wingless bipeds, especially when we are still at that stage of life when notions of accomplishment and making something of ourselves have yet to put the damper on just plain fooling around.

The transformation of pure play into competitive play—the ancient Greeks were Olympic champs at this—constituted one of the first such dampers. We went from pointless play to keeping one eye on the scoreboard. And our current dedication to sports as self-improvement, complete with personal trainers and strange garments made out of spandex, has virtually wiped out any lightheartedness remaining in play. Even when taking a walk, distance and elapsed time are now often recorded, then measured against previous records as we compete with ourselves for our personal best. Play is no longer something we do with our idle time; it is another ambitious activity crammed into our schedules.

This idea of losing oneself is fundamental to most uses of the word "play." When a person does some playacting, she loses herself in the part she is playing; indeed the whole enterprise is called "putting on a play." In play, we leap into the realm of imagination. Plato pointed out that "leaping" is at the root of many words for play; he believed that the desire to leap, as in leaping for joy, is basic to all leg-bearing animals, including humans. Inside our imaginations, we play out a fantasy—say, that we are a knight of the Round Table or that the fate of mankind depends on whether we beat the odds in a game of solitaire. And even when we play a game that has clear parameters—say, stickball—the rules of play are ultimately inconsequential: whether we win or lose, or even follow the rules to the letter or not, it has no serious consequences in the nonplay world; after all, it's just a game.

Of course, we also can lose ourselves in serious matters, such as work, but the critical distinction is that in nonplay activities we never lose our sense of purpose, our goal. We could, for example, lose ourselves in the activity of writing a business memo, but hovering over us throughout is the fact that we have to get it done, and done well, before the end of the business day. The only goal of pure play is itself. We do not even play *in order* to have fun; we simply have fun playing. Just ask a child or, for that matter, a talkative bear cub: he doesn't initiate play for the *purpose* of enjoyment, but he nonetheless has a dandy time doing it.

ON OLD MEN AT PLAY

My earliest memory of seeing old men happily at play was in Paris in the early sixties. At the time, I was taking graduate courses in philosophy at the Sorbonne, courses that would have baffled me in English let alone French, and I was feeling a bit lonely and pathetic in a late-adolescent, vaguely romantic, Parisian sort of way. Lugging around my seven-hundred-page copy of Jean-Paul Sartre's *L'être et le néant* (*Being and Nothingness*), I took moody walks, and on one of these I wandered through a stone archway in the fifth arrondissement that led into a park called the Arènes de Lutèce. In this nearly hidden spot, I came upon the remnants of the Romans' first-century outpost, complete with a mammoth amphitheater.

I climbed to the top of the gallery and sat. Below me, on the same ground where gladiators once played their lethal games, a group of six old Frenchmen were playing *pétanque*, a variation of the lawn-bowling game *boules*. What struck me immediately was the grace and decorum of these old guys: all wore Jackets and ties or cravats, some sported berets, and their demeanor with one another was both genteel—a finely executed bowl was acknowledged by the others with polite bows—and warmly familiar. They smiled and laughed frequently; they touched one another's backs and shoulders easily and often. But above all, this sextet of handsome, dignified old geezers played with gusto.

I found the spectacle deeply moving. For reasons that were not clear to me at the time, I was suddenly filled with a hopefulness that had been absent for so long I did not at first recognize it. The players' happiness floated up to me, embraced me. Looking back now, I believe that much of the exhilaration I felt came from the fact that these were *old* guys, at the far end of life from where I sat, yet they were still reveling in the joy of being alive. I cannot imagine anything that would have been more inspiring for a young man stepping unsteadily into adult life.

Was the joy that filled these old Frenchmen a result of their immersion in play or was the play an expression of the joy that already resided inside them, an outlet for that joy? This is the kind of question that philosophers and psychologists (and Huizinga) ask, but I am content simply to know that pure play and joy are intimately connected.

I am sure it was no coincidence that only days after watching that game of *pétanque* I withdrew from graduate school and set out to have as much fun as I could before my money ran out and I needed to return to the States to earn a living. Maybe it was the Epicurean in me: I was inspired to play. I may also have taken comfort in a neat piece of etymology that a wry Sorbonne classmate had recently taught me: in ancient Greek the original meaning of the word for school was "leisure." This classmate told me that Plato drove this idea home in his dialogue *Euthydemus*, in which Socrates puts down the Sophists, claiming that a man learns more by "playing" with ideas in his leisure time than by sitting in a classroom. And Plato's successor, that world champion of pleasure, Epicurus, believed in a simple yet elegant connection between learning and happiness: the entire purpose of education was to attune the mind and senses to the pleasures of life.

Enough said. I was outta there!

Only weeks after witnessing this game of *pétanque*, I was roaming the Spanish countryside and came upon a group of old men and young children harvesting almonds. Together they had spread blankets under an almond tree; then the youngsters jiggled the limbs of the tree with poles and rakes, shaking the hulls loose while the old men stood around the blankets' edges, kicking back fallen nuts that were skittering off them. It was a perfect division of labor: the very young jiggling vigorously, the very old kicking leisurely.

After watching them for a few minutes, I sensed a regular beat to their movements, a captivating cross rhythm of jiggles and kicks worthy of an Elvin Jones drum solo. And sure enough, a little later they all began to sing a folk song that I am sure had been sung for centuries by Spanish children and old men gathering almonds together, a song that matched the cadences of their movements.

Although the song was clearly well known to all of them, it burst from their throats with the spontaneity of, well, a leap of joy. They had transformed work into play and, as with all pure play, they had lost themselves in it. It was an act of communal transcendence, more uplifting in my view than the chanting of any hymn or prayer I ever heard in a synagogue or church. Listening to the almond pickers' song, my spirit soared.

Young children make natural playmates for old folks. We

have fabulous qualities in common that have gone missing from people in that sticky stage between immaturity and old age. For starters, we are both naturally into patient slowness. A little kid can spend hours unhurriedly repeating the same operation: say, constructing a tower out of building blocks, and when it totters and falls, giggling and starting all over again. In my old age, I can get into that one; I can easily lose myself in it. I am in no hurry to get that tower up there once and for all, as I was when I was a middle-aged father perpetually conscious of the pressing responsibilities that awaited me once I was done with this endless tower-building business. In those days, I might have even become frustrated by the utter futility of trying to get that tower up permanently; it would have smacked too much of Sisyphus and plunged me into existential angst. Not now. The goal—a fully erect tower—is only incidental to the game. In fact, when the tower collapses, I have a good laugh too. The kid and I are having unadulterated fun.

This natural affinity for slowness that young children and oldsters share tips over into shared intellectual games—yes, *intellectual* games. The little kid who asks his grandfather, "Why do birds fly?" or "Where do babies come from?" has come to the right person. An old man can get down on all fours for questions like these; he is in no hurry to get to conclusive answers. Both young and old alike sense that after the facts about wings and fertilized eggs have been dispensed with, they are still faced with some basic philosophical questions, say, about the purpose of a life (to fly?) and the ultimate beginnings of things (but where did the *first* egg come from?). They share the foundation of all philosophical inquiry: pure and playful wonder. That is why the child keeps asking "But why?" after every answer Gramps gives him, and why Gramps could happily keep trying to come up with answers until the sun goes down.

When I tell one of my favorite philosophical gags, it is always a little kid who laughs the loudest.

Andreas: What holds the world up?
Orestes: Atlas, of course.
Andreas: But what holds up Atlas?
Orestes: He stands on the back of a turtle.
Andreas: But what does the turtle stand on?
Orestes: On another turtle's back.
Andreas: But what does that turtle stand on?
Orestes: My dear Andreas, it's turtles all the way down!

A child gets the delicious absurdity of this dialogue about infinite regression better than anyone between our ages.

In my experience, friendly animals and old people also have a distinct commonality when it comes to pure play. There is a game I play with increasing frequency as I get older: rolling on the ground with my dog, Snookers. It brings me incalculable pleasure. I have yet to experience an unsatisfying roll-around with my doggie.

So how does it feel for this old guy to roll in the grass with his dog—or, to put it in Edmund Husserl's terms, what is the phenomenology of old-man-with-dog-rolling-in-the-grassness? (Leave it to a middle European philosopher to turn what personal essayists have been doing for time immemorial—recording how their experiences *feel*—into abstract scholarship.)

For starters, it feels silly. In fact, I feel so silly that I involuntarily start giggling. My giggling, in turn, makes Snookers jump on my torso and start to lick my face. I push him away playfully, which is to say, I do not entirely mean it, and Snookers knows this so he keeps on jumping and licking. We roll around some more. That's pretty much the whole game.

No doubt there is a physiological element to the way this game makes me feel—probably something to do with how the rolling and giggling affect the flow of blood to my brain—but be that as it may, what I feel is a kind of stoned lightness of being. I feel extraordinarily happy. If this is what second childhood is all about, I am glad to be here.

Now and then a neighbor will come upon Snookers and me rolling around. On these occasions, I believe I am afforded some latitude in their judgment due to my age. In any event, I am pleased to report that both Snookers and I keep a game face.

—m—

Of course, on a sunny day, all I need to do is look over at Tasso's table on Dimitri's terrace to recognize an old man's finest playmates: his old friends. Happily, back at home I have my own variant of Tasso's table.

Over thirty years ago, when we were still in our early forties, my friend Lee, a comedy writer, established a lunch club for funny guys. Optimistically—we should live so long—he dubbed the club the Old Farts. Lee envisioned a gathering akin to the Algonquin Round Table, but what inevitably evolved was a table of raucous gagsters.

We still gather ever few months in a low-rent restaurant and yak for hours. A serious subject may come up—say, the latest political scandal—but this only serves as the kickoff into a gag, and then another, a "topper," and then a topper of the topper: jokes upon jokes, many told in the old, unhurried style of our fathers, with lots of bizarre character development and digressive details so the jokes become nuanced, far-fetched stories, a sort of borscht-belt magic realism. The joking is only marginally competitive, although, of course, bad puns are booed so loudly that the waiter often becomes alarmed.

We old guys laugh ourselves silly.

What we are up to, according to Professor Huizinga's ranking, is one of the highest forms of human recreation: playing with words and ideas. Wit, funny stuff—taking the world into our imaginations, playing around with it, and then shamelessly passing off the absurd as the real.

ON THE ZENITH OF MY APPRECIATION
OF OLD MEN AT PLAY

It was a half decade after watching those young and old almond harvesters in the Spanish countryside when I first saw old Greek men dancing, a form of ecstatic play I had not witnessed before and have not seen so passionately performed since. I was still new to Hydra at the time and had not yet made the many friends, both Greek and expatriate, who were to enrich my life ever afterward.

Outside the window of my hillside house, a full moon had set the whitewashed houses and stone paths of Hydra aglow in what looked like a photo negative of the island's daytime landscape. What had appeared stark under the sun seemed spectral in the moonlight, and the unearthly light coming through my window drew me out of my room and down to the coastal walkway for a dreamy ramble. It was utterly quiet except for an occasional donkey bray and rooster crow, making me especially aware of the absence of background noise on the island. A place without motor vehicles redefines silence.

Then I heard music coming from the direction of the main port, at first only the stuttering beat of bass notes, then, as I walked toward the music, the Turkic twang of a bouzouki. I followed the sound to a taverna called Loulou's. By then I recognized the music; it was a classic song by Mikis Theodorakis, whose music was at the time prohibited by the ruling dictatorship because of his antifascist activities. The doors to Loulou's were locked shut, but one of the windows was unshuttered and open wide. I peered inside.

Five old men were dancing side by side, connected one to the other by handkerchiefs held in their raised hands. Their craggy faces were tilted upward with what struck me as pride, defiance, and, above all, exultation. All of them were straining to keep their backs erect, though none fully succeeded, yet their legs executed the dance's sideward steps in perfect, graceful synchrony. When, toward the end of the song, the music gradually accelerated, their steps accelerated along with it. For a long moment after the music's crescendo climax, they remained standing silently next to one another with upraised arms. No one shouted *oopa!* as I later learned was customary. What I had witnessed, quite simply, was a dance to life—to its endurance in spite of the totalitarian regime in Athens and, ultimately, in spite of the impediments of old age. This was play at its most exalted.

I fully understood what Plato meant when he stated that pure play has intimations of the divine. In his often-quoted section on playing in the *Laws*, he wrote: "Man is made God's plaything, and that is the best part of him. . . . Therefore every man and woman should live life accordingly, and play the noblest games. . . . What, then, is the right way of living? Life must be lived as play."

It turns out that since Plato a great number of philosophers, both major and minor, have weighed in on the metaphysical meaning of play, including the enigmatic twentieth-century German ontologist Martin Heidegger, who asked rather bafflingly in *The Principle of Reason*, "Must we think about Being . . . by beginning with the essence of play?"

Heidegger's question is too far out there for me, yet I do sense something deeply meaningful in this idea of all life being play. It is a worldview that treasures life while ultimately taking none of it totally seriously. This is not so much a cynical "it's all a big joke so nothing really matters" attitude as it is a sense that we can transcend ourselves in the play of our lives. Yes, we are players in a game we can never fully understand, yet what an astounding game it is.

ON PLAYING WITH TIME

"He flips each bead according to some rhythm inside him," Dimitri is saying as he gestures toward his father, Ianos, who gazes thoughtfully out the window as he plays with his *kombolói*. "He's like an orchestra conductor setting the tempo of his life."

If Dimitri's interpretation is right, there really may be something existentialist in playing with the *kombolói*. It is a way of attending to time itself, this "spacing it out" and "making it last." Maybe Ianos's practice of this old Greek tradition truly isn't a nervous pastime but quite the opposite: it is a way to capture time, to make it his own. He *plays* with time.

I ask Dimitri why, in his opinion, *kombolói* are dying out in Greece. He shrugs.

"Who knows?" he says. "We have become more European and less ourselves. It's not all bad—I grew up in fear of the *matiasma* [the evil eye]. I had to wear one of those blue bracelets to ward it off. I even wore it at sea all those years, and I got a lot of teasing for it. But now only old people still believe in the *matiasma*. To tell the truth, I don't miss all that hocus-pocus."

"But will you miss the *kombolói*?" I ask him.

"I still have my own," he replies. "I sometimes play with them, but only when I am alone. Maybe I'm a little embarrassed to use them in public now. But, yes, I will miss them when my father's generation goes and it becomes a forgotten thing." He laughs. "But maybe it won't. They are making a comeback with some Athenian yuppies—they use them to help themselves give up smoking. They come off the hydrofoil with *kombolói* in one hand and an iPhone in the other."

I have to laugh at that image. It sums up the tension between the two poles of "lived time" perfectly.

Memory is the mother of all wisdom.

———

—AESCHYLUS

Chapter Three

Tasso's Rain-Spattered Photographs

....

ON SOLITARY REFLECTION

....

Making my way back from Dimitri's to my room, I again see Tasso on his highest terrace and, minutes later, from the desk window of my room, I gaze over at him again. I now see that there is a small table beside him, on it some old notebooks and what appears to be a box of postcards and photographs. His craggy face seems both pensive and content. It is a day for solitary reflection.

Back in my room, I hear rain beginning to fall, pattering lightly on the tile roof over my head. I feel chilly, a bit lonely, and, well, particularly old. Executing a few exultant dance steps does not seem like the ticket at this particular moment. I retire to my narrow bed to read some more about the philosophies of boredom and play, my interim strategy for warding off the old-man rainy day blues. It feels like a good *kairós* for playing with ideas.

ON IDLE THOUGHTS

Svendsen points out that many early thinkers tied the idle life to the production of superior ideas and a deeper understanding of life. He cites the Roman poet Lucan, who wrote, "Leisure ever creates varied thought," and Montaigne, in his essay "Of Idleness," agrees wholeheartedly, adding that "like a horse that has broken from its rider," idle thought is far more adventurous than regimented thought. Svendsen also mentions the eighteenth-century German philosopher Johann Hamann, who believed that the idle have a better perspective on philosophical ideas than academics do, in part because they are less likely to get caught up in minutiae. He would get no argument from me on that. Apparently, Hamann could get a tad defensive on the subject of idleness: when a friend criticized him for loafing, he is said to have retorted that work is easy, but true idleness takes courage and fortitude.

True idleness also requires patience, which, in a sense, is the antidote for boredom. An authentic old man can be a master of patience for the simple reason that he is in no hurry for time to pass. I remember one long-ago evening, on an overcrowded train to Philadelphia, hearing a young woman moan to her mother, "God, I wish we were there already!" Her white-haired mother replied eloquently, "Darling, never wish away a minute of your life."

Even old age's lack of new experiences can be considered a boon. We've done "new" already, and usually found it wanting. Writes Svendsen, "Existential boredom . . . must fundamentally be understood on the basis of a concept of a dearth of accumulated experience. The problem is that we try to get beyond this boredom by piling on increasingly new and more potent sensations and impressions, instead of allowing ourselves to accumulate experience."

Yes, *accumulated experience*—that is precisely what an old person has available to him in abundance. The trick is to slow down enough that this accumulated experience can be contemplated and even, hopefully, savored.

ON THE SUPERIORITY OF MENTAL PLEASURES

Epicurus was convinced that mental pleasures surpass physical pleasures, largely because the mind has the advantage of being able to contemplate pleasures of the past and anticipate pleasures of the future. According to an explication by the Roman philosopher Cicero, a late-in-life Epicurean convert, this permitted "a continuous and interconnected [set of] pleasures."

From a modern psychological perspective, this Epicurean

ability of the mind to feel pleasure simply by remembering pleasant sensations seems exaggerated and overly optimistic. But nonetheless, Epicurus's enthusiasm for the joys of thought—particularly for solitary contemplation and enlightening conversation—remains worth thinking about.

Both Epicurus and Plato believed that old age provided a unique chance for unbounded, wide-ranging thought. In the *Republic*, Plato basically attributed this window of opportunity to the fact that we aren't that horny anymore: "Old age has a great sense of calm and freedom; when the passions relax their hold, then . . . we are freed from the grasp of not one mad master only but of many."

And Epicurus saw this opportunity of old age as one more benefit from leaving the world of commerce and politics behind us; it frees us to focus our brainpower on other matters, often more intimate and philosophical matters. Being immersed in the commercial world constrains the mind, limiting it to conventional, acceptable thought; it is hard to close a sale if we pause in the proceedings to meditate at length about man's relation to the cosmos. Furthermore, without a business schedule, we simply have the time to ruminate unhurriedly, to pursue a thought for as long and as far as it takes us. In a letter to Menoeceus, Epicurus noted that an old man is in an ideal position to open his mind to new ideas "in consequence of his absence of fear for the future." An old man does not have to fret about his next move because the chess game is over. He is free to think about any damned thing he chooses.

Contemporary brain research contributes a synaptic angle on Plato's observation that in old age we are in better shape for thinking philosophical thoughts. A study done at the Université de Montréal found that older minds are more efficient than younger ones. Writes the principal researcher of the study, Dr. Oury Monchi, "We now have neurobiological evidence showing that with age comes wisdom and that as the brain gets older, it learns to better allocate its resources." And research undertaken at the University of California, San Diego, found that "a slower brain may be a wiser brain" because in old age those parts of the brain identified with abstract, philosophical thought and with perceptual anticipation are freed from the distracting effects of the neurotransmitter dopamine. "The elderly brain is less dopamine-dependent, making people less impulsive and controlled by emotion," the study concluded. Aha! So dopamine is Plato's "mad master"!

I am not completely comfortable with letting scientists define what we mean by "wiser," yet I do remain convinced that old people have the capacity to think from a perspective that is substantially *different* from that of their younger selves. This may be because topics more suited to slow thinking come along with thinking slowly, or because an old person simply has more time for contemplation, or because—who knows?—he has been liberated from his dopamine addiction. Whatever the root of his new ways of thinking, he now has the opportunity to think about some fascinating things.

ON THE AUTOBIOGRAPHICAL URGE

We old people often like to think about the accumulated experiences of our lives. In that same deathbed letter to Menoeceus, Epicurus wrote, "When a man is old, he may be young in good things through the pleasing recollection of the past." It reminds me of an expression I heard a neighbor use when I was a child: "That woman's so old she can be any age she wants to be."

But sometimes an old person wants to do more than just randomly recollect things past; he (or she) wants to search for a thread in his life, something that holds it together as his.

ON AUTOBIOGRAPHY AND
AUTHENTIC OLD AGE

The autobiographical impulse comes in two models. The first is the currently surging urge to pass along the story of our lives to others: the recent bulge in the over-sixty-five population has yielded an abundance of published memoirs. The second model is simply to get the story of our lives straight for *ourselves*. These often turn out to be conflicting impulses. An inherent problem in writing one's memoirs for others to read is the temptation to indulge in literary nips and tucks. After all, who really wants to be remembered as, say, a man who spent an inordinate amount of time watching *Law & Order*? Not for publication! But just possibly the fact that a man spent many an hour intrigued by *Law & Order* does figure in an honest attempt to make thematic sense of the life he lived. For the philosophically minded, the venture of constructing one's life story for oneself alone figures prominently in the making of an authentic old age.

But some philosophers disapprove. In the second book of his *Rhetoric*, Aristotle, a dedicated curmudgeon on the subject of old folks, wrote: "They live by memory rather than by hope; for what is left to them of life is but little as compared with the long past; and hope is of the future, memory of the past. This, again, is the cause of their loquacity; they are continually talking of the past, because they enjoy remembering it."

To say the least, this is not a rousing recommendation to follow the autobiographical urge.

Bertrand Russell takes up Aristotle's argument more tellingly. Russell, a precocious forever youngster who lived to the age of ninety-eight (he attributed his longevity to having chosen his ancestors carefully), wrote in his 1975 essay "How to Grow Old": "Psychologically there are two dangers to be guarded against in old age. One of these is undue absorption in the past. It does not do to live in memories, in regrets for the good old days, or in sadness about friends who are dead. One's thoughts must be directed to the future, and to things about which there is something to be done."

And in the poem "Why Should Not Old Men Be Mad?"

William Butler Yeats describes what he saw as the inevitable product of dwelling on the past—a personal docudrama of failed expectations:

> *Why should not old men be mad?*
> *Some have known a likely lad*
> *That had a sound fly fisher's wrist*
> *Turn to a drunken journalist;*
> *A girl that knew all Dante once*
> *Live to bear children to a dunce;*
> . . . .
> *No single story would they find*
> *Of an unbroken happy mind,*
> *A finish worthy of the start.*
> *Young men know nothing of this sort,*
> *Observant old men know it well;*
> *And when they know what old books tell*
> *And that no better can be had,*
> *Know why an old man should be mad.*

But I find myself more persuaded by the psychologist and existentialist philosopher Erik Erikson, who was convinced that memories laced with regret and despair are not our only option. On the contrary, Erikson says, mature and wise ways of reminiscing are precisely what we need in an authentic old age.

ON THE AUTOBIOGRAPHICAL IMPERATIVE

One of Erikson's most highly regarded contributions to modern psychology was his formulation of stages of personal evolution that go beyond the traditional Freudian stages of early childhood development to include all of life, including old age. This last, he encouragingly called "maturity."

In each stage, Erikson posited a polar tension that needs to be resolved to get successfully through it. For example, in young adulthood the primary tension is between intimacy and isolation. A successful resolution follows from forming loving relationships with others, while an unsuccessful outcome is loneliness and alienation. In maturity Erikson sees the tension between what he calls "ego integrity" and despair. The fundamental task of this stage is *to reflect back on one's life.*

For Erikson, a successful resolution of the tension between ego integrity and despair is a wise and considered sense of fulfillment, a philosophical acceptance of oneself in spite of serious mistakes and stumbles along the way. Erickson believed that a philosophical acceptance of one's life in old age stemmed directly from a matured capacity for love. He wrote that the key personal relationship in a successful navigation through old age is with, of all people, mankind—which he dubs "my kind"—the ultimate family relationship. An unsuccessful outcome of reflecting back on one's life is unmitigated regret and bitterness.

So in Erikson's philosophy it turns out that this old-age impulse to find a narrative thread to our lives is more than just an indulgence in ruefulness or idle daydreaming—it is critical stuff. This is what Svendsen is suggesting when he writes that "accumulated experience" is the opposite of, and quite possibly the best relief from, the boredom of living one isolated and unconnected experience after another. Tying our experiences together in a personal history is a way we find meaning in our lives.

ON CHERRY-PICKING MEMORIES

Charles Dickens begins his masterwork *David Copperfield*, "Whether I shall turn out to be the hero of my own life, or whether that station will be held by anybody else, these pages must show."

That line always brings a smile to my face. After all, if I am not the hero of my own life, who the hell else could it be? But I suspect that old Dickens was setting up a proto-existentialist gag here: that "anybody else" could be the personification of the outside powers that determined the events in Copperfield's life, say, fate. To put it another way, maybe David Copperfield did not *choose* his life; he just let it happen to him. The existentialists would not approve. Whether or not Copperfield turns out to be the *subjective* hero of his life is the fundamental question that the first-person narrator apparently hopes to answer by recounting his adventures in "these pages." This pursuit begins by asking what events appear to be meaningful and to follow meaning-fully from other events.

Even when we are only composing memoirs for ourselves alone, we still cherry-pick our memories, choosing those that give some semblance of a neat narrative line to our personal histories, some sense of cause and effect, even of personal growth. And, then, of course there is that other nasty problem, which Mark Twain eloquently noted: "When I was younger I could remember anything, whether it happened or not; but I am getting old, and soon I shall remember only the latter." It seems, after all, that we'll need to take a look at that pesky philosophical question, "How do we know what is real and true?" although gently qualified by the addendum, "Does it really make much difference in this case?"

When we reminisce for our own private gratification, we usually do not seek out a fact-checker. What we are interested in is recalling an *experience*: how it felt to us, what it meant to us then, and what it means to us now. For example, whether I actually did have a particular conversation about wild strawberries with Professor Erikson back in college, or I am confounding it with a conversation I had with a classmate, or possibly only even had inside my head after attending an Erikson lecture, would not seem to make a determinate difference in putting together a meaningful story of my life. What *may* matter, and perhaps a great deal, is that the subject of this conversation—whether or not it actually occurred—was something that had a memorable impact on me, perhaps on the development of a lifetime interest, possibly even on my subsequent worldview. Indeed the fact that I have this memory and attach significance to it matters more than its absolute, objective truth.

No, I am not wandering off into a la-la land where I claim a memory is true simply because I *think* it is true. If I vividly recall my first moon walk as an astronaut, despite having it on good authority that I was never an astronaut and never came closer to the moon than the peak of Mount Washington, I will have to say that I have waited too long to meditate on the story of my life and have crossed the border into *old* old age where I simply cannot think straight. Somewhere between my possibly misremembered conversation with Professor Erikson and a moon walk fantasy-memory, I will need to draw a line. Not easy.

A series of lectures on the art of memoir held at the New York Public Library was called Inventing the Truth. Cute, but they were also on to something important with that title: when we try to put together our life story, we seek out patterns and themes, and that, in turn, determines which memories make the cut. And, of course, the other way around too: we sift through our memories for themes and then search for memories that validate them.

In our way, we are attempting to pull off the same artful trick that Dickens did: by picking and choosing scenes from our lives, we are trying to give it coherence, even—heaven help us—*meaning*. But arbitrary as our choices may be, they are all that is available to us for this task. In his five-pound magnum opus *Being and Nothingness*, Sartre wrote: "There is a magic in recollection. . . . In remembering we seem to attain that impossible synthesis . . . that life yearns for."

In a philosophical old age, there is nothing I yearn for more than that impossible synthesis.

ON THE WISDOM OF *WILD STRAWBERRIES*

Toward the end of his popular course The Human Life Cycle, given at Harvard in the 1960s, Erikson would pull down the shades in his lecture hall and show Ingmar Bergman's classic film *Wild Strawberries*. Erikson said that no case history or psychological survey captured the "overall coherence, the 'gestalt,' of a whole life" as well as this film. He considered it an extraordinarily sensitive and evocative modern portrayal of an old man reviewing his life and attempting both to make sense of it and come to terms with it.

It is easy for me to understand why Erikson found so much richness in *Wild Strawberries*. The film traces a single long day of travel, memories, dreams, presentiments, and encounters with family members and strangers in the life of a retired Swedish doctor and bacteriologist, Dr. Isak Borg. In the company of his daughter-in-law, who is currently estranged from his son, Borg drives to Lund University, where he is to receive a medal for fifty years of dedication to his profession. At the beginning of this journey, he is an embittered old man, isolated and cynical in the extreme about the consolations of religion and the possibility that his, or any, life could have some transcendent meaning.

Before his journey even begins, Borg is forced to confront the imminence of his death in a chilling dream of a clock without hands and a runaway horse-drawn hearse, which is revealed to contain his own corpse. The shadow of his mortality follows him for the rest of the day, compelling him to attempt one last time to make some kind of sense of his life. It is an extremely painful process for Borg.

Many of the memories that come to him, especially of his childhood, are virtually indistinguishable from his dreams, and, dreamlike, these memories are distorted by his emotions, particularly by his pervasive feeling of regret. Do these distortions make his memories any less real? Or do they highlight the significance of the memories for him? For Erikson, both of these questions miss Bergman's striking insight that we are able to "invent the truth" of our memories by the wisdom we bring to bear on them. Regret is not the only lens through which Borg can see his life.

But regret cannot be dismissed either. This is not a feel-good film in which Borg, in the end, concludes that all in all he actually made a pretty good go of it. Not at all. Still, by day's end Borg does achieve a redemption of sorts. He accepts his life, regrets and all, as *his own*—a human life, a life deeply connected to "my kind." And he painfully reaches out to the people around him.

The Italian director Federico Fellini's classic life-review film *8½* tackles the question of regrets more directly and perhaps less subtly than *Wild Strawberries*, not to mention more light-heartedly, even comically. Living near the Mediterranean will do that to a man. In *8½* the central character, Guido, a film-maker bereft of inspiration, finds himself reminiscing about the people and events in his life; these memories, in turn, become his sought-after film. Along the way, Guido has to contend with the comments of a cynical Greek chorus in the form of his arch-critic, Daumier. Says Daumier, "What a monstrous presumption to believe that others might profit by the squalid catalog of your mistakes. And what good would it do to yourself to piece together the shreds of your life, your vague memories . . . ?"

Yet by the end of his journey, Guido is ecstatic bordering on manic: "Everything is just as it was before. Everything is confused again, but this confusion is *me*! . . . I am not afraid anymore of admitting that I seek and have not yet found. Only this way can I feel alive, only this way can I look into your eyes without shame. . . . Accept me as I am if you can. It is the only way we really have to find ourselves."

———

The conversation I believe I had with Professor Erikson was about the ending of *Wild Strawberries*. I was twenty at the time and generally angry at the world, as many of us were in the early 1960s. I could not even begin to imagine what it would be like to be an old man looking back on my life, but this did not deter me from saying to my teacher, "Wasn't it a little late for Borg to try to connect to other people? After all, most of his life was over." And Professor Erikson replied, simply, "He still had time."

—⁓—

I get up from my bed and walk slowly to my desk window. Tasso has withdrawn from his terrace, but I am still able to see him inside his house, sitting at a table almost directly across from me. He is blotting raindrops off an old photograph with the sleeve of his shirt.

Man is condemned to be free;
because once thrown into the world, he is
responsible for everything he does.

———————

—JEAN-PAUL SARTRE

Chapter Four

A Sirocco of Youth's Beauty

ON EXISTENTIAL AUTHENTICITY

There is a hot wind blowing today, streaming up from Africa by way of Crete. It is neither fiery nor powerful enough to qualify as a sirocco (in Greek, *sirókos*), but that does not prevent the islanders from claiming that they are being stirred by the "*sirókos* effect"—hot tempers and intemperate passions. This is said to be the result of the dissonance caused by one's nerves expecting, as usual, to be cooled by a wind but instead being heated by it. From my seat at Dimitri's, not all the doors I hear slamming are caused by the wind.

Some islanders, like Tasso, are pretty sure that many people use the *sirókos* effect as an excuse for indulging in a tirade or some uninhibited sex. But Tasso, for one, is not likely to bring this analysis to anyone's attention. He once told me that he believes the so-called *sirókos* effect provides a welcome catharsis that keeps the body politic in balance in the same way that the excesses of Carnaval prepare Brazilians to endure the deprivations of Lent. I am sure Tasso was once a broad-minded, enlightened judge.

He and his friends are again seated at their table, chatting amiably, so far exclusively about the weather and what it portends. Then quite abruptly, they all go quiet. To a man, they are gazing up at the top step of the stone stairs that lead down from the coast path and past the taverna's terrace. A young woman has appeared there, and the wind is pressing her blouse and skirt against her splendid, voluptuous body. For a moment, she pauses there, perhaps enjoying the warm breeze, but more likely enjoying the effect she is having on the men looking up at her—her personal *sirókos*-effect indulgence. A few seconds later another woman appears, an older woman swathed in the traditional black garments of a reverent widow. She sizes up the situation immediately and brusquely grasps the young woman's arm and leads her down the steps. The young woman is named Elena. She is nineteen years old and is a classic Greek beauty with lustrous jet-black hair; clear, light olive skin; and large, dark, flashing eyes. The matron is her grandmother.

The old men unabashedly keep their eyes on Elena as she and her grandmother draw near to where they are sitting. When Elena and the old woman are directly in front of them, all the men rise slightly from their chairs and greet them. While saying, "Good day," Tasso offers an elegant bow from his none-too-supple waist. It is clearly a bow of admiration and gratitude for Elena's beauty.

A moment later, grandmother and granddaughter gone, the conversation at Tasso's table resumes, but it is no longer about the weather. Flushed and animated, the men talk about beautiful women they have seen and known in their lives. Tasso takes the lead this time; he has traveled the most and married later than his companions. He begins by declaring that there is nothing more beautiful than a *young* woman and that is because youth itself is incomparable in its beauty. There is more than a hint of the philosopher-poet about Tasso on this subject. I am reminded of a friend of mine who, in a similar situation, riffed on Keats, saying, "Youth is beauty and beauty is youth."

ON SEXUAL URGES VERSUS
SEXUAL NOSTALGIA

Once word got out that prostitutes were welcome at Epicurus's table, a rumor spread in Athens that behind the Garden's walls, they were conducting orgies of, well, epicurean proportions. But the gossip could not have been further from the truth.

On the topic of sex, Epicurus was even less of what is now

thought of as an epicurean, because sex, he believed, had a tendency to get out of hand, to skitter outside the all-important comfort zone. Marriage and procreation, yes, these provide lasting satisfactions (although Epicurus himself never married), but sex—and purely sexual love—inevitably leads to more unhappiness than its fleeting pleasures are worth. Sex exposes unnecessary and insatiable needs that bare vulnerabilities and promote anxieties. Epicurus mapped out the sequence in which sex causes misery: it starts with lust, moves on to ardor, peaks with consummation, and then goes directly to jealousy or boredom or both. No comfort for Epicurus there.

And not much there that I believe would resonate with Tasso and his friends or, for that matter, with me. For the likes of us, sex was usually well worth its headaches, even as we look back on it now—perhaps *especially* as we look back on it now. I am not suggesting that any of us are "dirty old men," still preoccupied with sexual fantasies and future exploits. The closest Tasso comes to that is when he confesses to his friends that for a brief moment while gazing at Elena at the top of the stone stairway he felt a tingling in his groin; said Tasso, smiling, "The sleeping giant awakened. But then he yawned and went back to sleep." No, I will leave such lusty, virile fantasies to my seventy-three-year-old friend who wears a testosterone patch and consumes seventy-two-hour Cialis.

ON EXISTENTIAL AUTHENTICITY

Thinking again about this forever youngster with the testosterone patch helps me sort out my evolving philosophy of a good and authentic old age. It is one thing to have an active libido but a listless phallus; in that case Cialis seems like a perfectly wonderful solution. But it is quite another to don a testosterone patch for the express purpose of *reactivating* one's libido. The latter amounts to wanting to want something that you currently don't want. And that is a very peculiar mind-set in which to be.

Jean-Paul Sartre, the twentieth-century existentialist who seems to have taken up a perch on my shoulder alongside Epicurus, provides a compelling way to look at this "forever young" conundrum. In Sartrean ethics we are directed to live authentically—"authenticity" being Sartre's take on the almost universally accepted injunction "To thine own self be true." A person lives authentically if he operates from the principle that his existence precedes his essence. He is not *essentially*, say, a waiter or a Democrat or a daytime drinker; these are roles he may *choose* to play, but not innate qualities that he cannot transcend. For example, an authentic person cannot in good faith say, "I drink two scotches at lunch simply because that is just the way I am." He would be treating himself as an object with immutable characteristics, not existing as a subject with the ability to choose who he is and what actions he takes.

For me, the most relevant piece here is Sartre's warning against treating oneself as an object. This is a rare bit of moral philosophy that I can actually *feel*: treating myself as an object makes me feel less alive, less myself. When, say, I find myself in the frame of mind where I am convinced that I am *essentially* an inconsiderate person and there's nothing to be done about it, I not only feel defeated, I feel that in denying my ability to will-fully change I have stopped being truly alive. But at the same time it would be ridiculous not to accept what is beyond my control: I can no more choose to be a young man than I can choose to be tall and blue eyed.

Basically, most of us want to be as responsible for our lives as we can be—it is fundamental to making our lives our own. I choose, therefore I am who I am. So if in old age a man finds himself well past the period when he is perpetually "on the make," is it authentic for him to infuse himself with testosterone so he can feel like someone he is not—namely, a horny young man? Wouldn't that be turning himself into an object—in this case some kind of sexual object?

I suppose a testosterone patch advocate could argue that the hormone supplement will not turn him into someone else but will simply add vigor and vitality to who he is now, much as an energy drink might. In fact, he may even contend that *choosing* to become horny again is a supreme act of self-creation, the height of authenticity.

Maybe. But I keep thinking that there are discrete stages of life, each with its own qualities, and that fudging these stages is to fudge the inherent value of each of them. It feels more authentic to me to recognize that human desires and capabilities change from one period of life to the next, and that to deny that they do is to miss out on what is most fulfilling about each stage. I am not about to try out for the role of the local young lothario; that would make about as much sense as trying out for third baseman in the local Little League—even if I were on steroids.

Why Cialis, yes, but testosterone, no? I admit I am making a somewhat arbitrary distinction here—generously, Sartre leaves loads of room for arbitrary distinctions—but taking Cialis seems more like getting treatment for a broken bone, so to speak, while the testosterone patch seems like tampering with what makes a man who he is at this particular point in his life. His libido isn't broken; it has run its natural course. Wanting to want something that he doesn't really want that much, and in his eighth decade, no less, just seems counterfeit, untrue to himself.

I don't know what to make of my sixty-eight-year-old friend who had her bosom beautified. Heaven knows, her surgeon did an impressive job. This friend told me that she now feels younger and more attractive, both of which make her happier, and it is always hard to argue with happiness.

ON EXISTENTIAL DENIAL

This testosterone patch/breast implant business is more than just an example of a typical "forever young" decision; it is emblematic of the entire enterprise of denying old age.

For the existentialists, as well as for most contemporary psychotherapists, there is nothing more deadly than the denial of the truth about our lives. A person living in denial is said to be not fully and truly alive, like the clueless denizens of Plato's cave, who mistake the shadows on the cave's wall for reality, while the facts of life—some hard to take—are vividly illuminated just outside the cave's wall.

Søren Kierkegaard, considered the father of existentialism, declared that man's ultimate denial is of the fact that he is mortal. We construct any number of death-denial strategies to avoid confronting this fact, from believing in an eternal afterlife to convincing ourselves that we will somehow "live on" through, say, our recently completed book of intimate poems. We do this for a perfectly understandable reason: the idea that we will die one day, never to live again, fills us with terror. But the alternative, Kierkegaard says, is to not wholly and genuinely live the one life we were given. Instead we clunk around in a cave of illusion.

In the mid-twentieth century, the anthropologist Ernest Becker further developed Kierkegaard's thesis in his Pulitzer Prize–winning work, *The Denial of Death*. Becker added a psychological and cultural dimension to death denial, seeing it as mankind's basic survival mechanism. Without this illusion, he argues, civilization would dissolve in despair. Becker believed that in this age of reason, when our hold on religious beliefs is tenuous, our failed attempt at grappling with mortality is the fundamental cause of the current upsurge of mental illness.

Denying that we are old is certainly not anywhere close, in order of magnitude, to denying that we are mortal, yet the two denials are clearly related. According to a recent survey, roughly half of Americans do *not* believe in an afterlife or any other form of immortality, the percentage of these nonbelievers increasing significantly among the more educated and affluent. Be that as it may, many of the forever young seem to be in denial that their personal expiration date is coming up soon. The result is that they do some fuzzy arithmetic when scheduling the rest of their lives. They figure they have loads of time to stay young, to remain in their go-get-'em stage of life.

But it doesn't add up that way. Because what happens then is that we proceed directly from the "forever young" stage of life to *old* old age, missing forever the chance at being a fulfilled old man "docked in the harbor, having safeguarded his true happiness." We lose out for eternity on what I am beginning to agree with Epicurus is the pinnacle of life.

Kierkegaard and Becker would probably see a death-denial strategy hidden in the denial of old age. After all, one thing about the old-man stage of life is that it is the *last* stage—that is, not counting *old* old age, when we are barely alive. By skipping old age we can easily forget that we really are in the final stage of life.

So opting for the "forever young" route may turn out to be a tricky death-denial strategy after all: our defense system figures out that if we forgo old age, we might be able to give the slip to our consciousness of our mortality. Yes, Kierkegaard's admonition to acknowledge our mortality is addressed to people of all ages, but the forever young, like genuinely young people, believe they will have plenty of time to think about it later.

ON FRANK SINATRA AND A WISTFUL OLD AGE

The warm wind appears to have run its course, but Tasso and his companions are still reminiscing about past loves. The vivaciousness that was initiated by Elena's appearance at the top of the stone steps has settled into a more lyrical mood. There is bittersweetness in the air.

Even as a young man, Francis Albert Sinatra, a.k.a. "Old Blue Eyes," had an uncommon gift for expressing the phenomenon of looking back at the joys and sorrows of past romances from the vantage point of a meditative and wistful old age. He conveyed nostalgia of the highest order, a nostalgia worthy of our attention. Like the European balladeers of his era—Jacques Brel, Edith Piaf, Gilbert Bécaud—Sinatra inhabited his songs.

And especially as he grew older and his voice rawer, no one ever doubted that Sinatra was singing from personal experience. He knew whereof he crooned.

I am thinking of the song "Once Upon a Time" (by Lee Adams and Charles Strouse), on Sinatra's quintessential "looking back" album, *September of My Years*:

> *Once upon a time*
> *A girl with moonlight in her eyes*
> *Put her hand in mine*
> *And said she loved me so,*
> *But that was once upon a time*
> *Very long ago.*

And later in the lyric:

> *Once upon a time*
> *The world was sweeter than we knew.*
> *Everything was ours,*
> *How happy we were then.*
> *But somehow once upon a time*
> *Never comes again.*

Sentimental stuff? You bet. But I have never been of the opinion that philosophy and sentiment—even sentimentality—

do not mix. In fact it is the estrangement of ordinary human emotions from philosophy that has made much of contemporary academic philosophy irrelevant to many of us.

Sinatra is sharing with us how it feels to recall being a young man blissful with love and hope. He relives his feelings from those years and, by God, they were absolutely wonderful. Yet it does an old man good to realize that was then and this is now. What remains, the memory of young love as seen through the filter of subsequent experience, has a sweetness of its own. The singer reminds us that we have lived through this period of intense, sometimes tempestuous emotions, and our lives feel richer for it. Not the least of it is that we have lived through those astonishing loves and heartbreaks and we are still here.

When Sinatra sings that "once upon a time never comes again," he manages to convey both the sorrow in the fact that this former stage of life can never be repeated and relief that this is so. He appears to be saying, "Those days were astonishing, yet I don't think I could handle that tempestuousness now— actually, I don't even think I'd *want* to now." And in this he is very clearly acknowledging his mortality: once upon a time *never* comes again.

While Kierkegaard would have us face death straight in the face and tremble with fear, Sinatra would have us offer a mournful nod to the face of death while at the same time wistfully extracting pleasure from our recollections of the sweetness in our younger lives. I am not convinced that Kierkegaard's acknowledgement of his mortality is any more authentic than Sinatra's.

ON ROMANTIC PLEASURES
RESERVED FOR OLD AGE

We find the same bittersweet appreciation of the poetic consciousness of old age when Sinatra sings the Alec Wilder and Bill Engvick classic "I See It Now":

That world I knew is lost to me
Loves have come and gone
The years go racing by
I live as best I can
And all at once I know it means the making of a man
I see it now
I see it now

The "making of a man": the accumulation of vivid experiences and the opportunity to look back upon them with both wonder and gratitude.

And in the ballad "This is All I Ask," by Gordon Jenkins, Sinatra puts an aging boulevardier's spin on Plato's appreciation of the "calm and freedom; when the passions relax their hold":

Beautiful girls,
Walk a little slower

When you walk by me.
Lingering sunsets,
Stay a little longer
With the lonely sea.

Like Tasso and his companions, Sinatra is still entranced by the sight of a beautiful woman, but now he can appreciate her beauty more purely, more aesthetically, than in his younger life, and that is because her beauty puts no demands on him. He is not compelled to chat her up, to initiate a seduction. For one thing, that is no longer an option for him—and, yes, there is something terribly sad about this. But now to simply and freely behold this beauty in front of him is refined enchantment, a pleasure reserved for old age. This is all he asks.

ON THE GRATIFICATIONS
OF BEING MARRIED IN OLD AGE

Neither Epicurus nor Plato devoted a great number of recorded thoughts to the subject of marriage. It was necessary for procreation, and procreation was natural and good, but beyond that these philosophers don't appear to have much of interest to say on the subject. Plato's student Aristotle even went so far as to argue that only men and women who would be *likely to have children together* should be allowed to be united in wedlock. (One does have to wonder how Aristotle would have determined that likelihood; after all, we all come from a long line of fertile ancestors.) Different times these were, including the fact that Plato, like many others in his culture, appeared to enjoy gay sex more than heterosexual sex; and since gay marriage was not an option at the time, this probably put a crimp in his philosophical thoughts about wedlock.

But even if Aristotle stressed utility over sentiment in his appraisal of marriage, he clearly appreciated the companionship it provided, a quality that grows in significance as a couple reaches old age. Wrote Aristotle: "Between man and wife friendship seems to exist by nature; for man is naturally inclined to form couples—even more than to form cities, inasmuch as the household is earlier and more necessary than the city." Then again, Aristotle, who apparently never met an old man he liked, wrote in Book II of his *Rhetoric* that the old "neither love warmly nor hate bitterly, but following the hint of Bias they love as though they will some day hate and hate as though they will some day love." Aristotle is said to have had a warm relationship with his second wife (his first wife died) up into his sixties, a ripe old age in those days, but one does have to wonder how his love-hate paradox played out around the family hearth.

Succeeding philosophers had a great deal to say about both the value and pitfalls of marriage, although few commented on a union that endures into old age. The big Christian thinkers viewed the married state less as a utilitarian enterprise than a sacrament, even if they qualified this sacrament as the only acceptable option for dealing with one's lust. Wrote Saint Augustine, "Abstinence from all sexual union is better even than marital intercourse performed for the sake of procreating." In other words, if you cannot control yourself, get married, but for heaven's sake don't enjoy it.

Since Saint Augustine, many philosophers have weighed in on the subject of wedlock, primarily as just one social contract among many others in a well-functioning state. In his *Metaphysics of Morals*, Kant attempts to reconcile his imperative not to treat others as objects with what happens when two people bind themselves in matrimony: "While one person is acquired by the other *as if it were a thing*, the one who is acquired acquires the other in turn; for in this way each reclaims itself and restores its personality." It is a sort of "turnabout is fair play" argument. And, of course, contemporary feminist philosophers have focused on marriage as the fundamental way that men limit women's freedom; the feminist Shulamith Firestone goes so far as to argue that women would do better to opt for nonmonogamy or lesbian separatism.

To my surprise, I find the most relevant commentary on a marriage that continues into the sunset years comes from the radical German philosopher Friedrich Nietzsche, who, in an atypically practical frame of mind, wrote, "When marrying, ask yourself this question: Do you believe that you will be able to converse well with this person into your old age? Everything else in marriage is transitory."

Who would have thought that at heart that nutty nihilist Nietzsche was actually a marriage counselor?

—⁓—

I know from a private conversation with Tasso that he has always loved being married, and now in old age he particularly values the unique companionship marriage offers. I do also. Although both of us married relatively late in our lives, by now each of us has been married for a very long time. We agree that a long marriage provides one of old age's greatest consolations, in no small part because as the marriage ages, the number of shared memories increases.

On Dimitri's terrace, Tasso is now telling the story of the first day he saw Sophia, his wife of forty-two years and the mother of his three children. He says the sunlight followed her like a spotlight as she strolled by him on Konstantinoupoleos Avenue just as he was leaving his office. He tells his friends that often when he looks at Sophia at breakfast in the morning, he sees that beautiful young woman strolling down Konstantinoupoleos Avenue.

Sing it, Frankie!

He who says either that the time for philosophy
has not yet come or that it has passed is like
someone who says that the time for happiness
has not yet come or that it has passed.

————

—EPICURUS

Chapter Five

The Tintinnabulation of Sheep Bells

ON MELLOWING TO METAPHYSICS

With a bag of books slung over my shoulder, I am walking the ancient mountainside road to the tiny village of Vlihos, a few miles west of Kamini, where I am lodging. During my first long stay on the island, in my twenties, this was a fifteen-minute stroll; now, factoring in my rest stops, it takes close to an hour. I imagine that the brisk stride of my youth felt more invigorating than my current puttering pace. There was a sense of urgency to everything I did as a young man—the general urgency of youth. I can imagine a forever youngster jogging past me in collegiate shorts and T-shirt, full of youthful, or at least *youthlike*, vigor. He would definitely get to Vlihos before me. But I am not in a hurry today. I am a contentedly dawdling old man.

For the second respite on my walk, I perch on a granite slab that offers a panoramic view of a grassy valley where sheep are safely grazing. I now become conscious of the faint tintinnabulation of the sheeps' bells, a plainsong from another era. A few moments pass and another sound joins the bells, scattered bursts, sharper, higher up on the treble scale, like a flute capriccio in a Vaughan Williams pastorale; it is the insistent call of a migrant babbler bird. A dog barks from somewhere down in Kamini and is quickly answered by a donkey's bray in the mountain above me—the horn section. I set down my bag, light up a cigarette, and listen.

Yes, I smoke—shamelessly. Back home in America, I have to endure insulting looks and comments—often from perfect strangers—when I light up. It is more than the scourge of secondhand smoke that offends these people; it is what they see as my perverse self-destructiveness. They are right, of course; tobacco is undoubtedly bad for my health and will probably shorten my life. As a defensive response to their comments, I often say, "Hey, I'm too old to die young."

Not exactly brilliant repartee, but it does make some personal sense to me. Like many men at my stage of life, I routinely scan the obituary page to find the age at which people are dying these days. Most often, it is in their seventies and eighties, the latter usually after a "long illness." If a person dies in his fifties or younger, this is sometimes labeled an "untimely death," and if I am in a Kierkegaardian frame of mind, I grimace at that description: *all* deaths are untimely compared to immortality; the exact age of a death is just a quibble.

Nonetheless, when I was younger, say in my fifties, I would shudder at the obits' reminder that in all probability I only had twenty-odd years left. And, because obituaries are usually devoted to people of noteworthy accomplishment, I would go into a panic—I only had twenty-odd years left to make something of myself!

But much to my surprise, when I, at the age of seventy-three, read the obituary of a man who passed away at the age of, say, seventy-five, I actually find it consoling. I have lived to a respectable old age. I have enjoyed the privilege of a complete life, partaking in all its stages (except, of course, *old* old age, which I would not mind skipping). When I read the obits now, Epicurus's dictum that the happiest life is free from self-imposed demands of commerce and politics strikes me anew. The "mad master" of "making it" has finally released me. I can savor the privilege of having lived to an old age. I am too old to die young.

That word, "privilege," has a special resonance for me. When my father-in-law, Jan Vuijst, a Dutch Reformed minister, was on his deathbed, I had a deeply intimate conversation with him—

as it turned out, my last conversation with him. He said to me, "It was a privilege to have lived." The soulful gratitude of that simple statement will never leave me.

ON THE FOLLY OF DENYING PLEASURE
IN OLD AGE

As it happens, smoking brings me pleasure and, at times like this, atop my granite roost on the Vlihos road, *great* pleasure. For that matter, so does a cheeseburger with a side of french fries and some mayonnaise in which to dip them. No doubt about it, these pleasures are bad for my health—very bad. I also have no doubt that a dedicated forever youngster forsakes these pleasures for this very reason; he has devoted himself to good health habits, especially now that he is in his midseventies. Yes, I can easily imagine him jogging past me, and I readily admit that he may take pleasure in his jog, not the least of which is the feeling of youthful vigor it yields to him. To each his own. But I do have to say that I am really enjoying this cigarette.

Perhaps I am guilty of some fuzzy arithmetic myself, but I have to wonder if the forever youngster's scrupulous health habits and the self-deprivations they undoubtedly involve will add an appreciable number of years to his robust old age or just prolong his *old* old age of merciless decay. Impossible to predict. But I am still left with the question of how many pleasures I am willing to forgo, never to enjoy again, in the name of longevity.

If not these pleasures now, when? In the do-not-resuscitate ward of the *old* old folks' home?

Corny old joke: An elderly man and his wife die in an airplane accident and up go to heaven. An angel welcomes them and starts showing them around. The man gets hungry and asks if they may get something to eat. The angel points to a lavish buffet of pâtés, cheeses, ribbed steaks, and creamy desserts and says, "Sure, help yourself. You can eat as much as you like and you don't need to have any health concerns." As they walk up to the buffet, the husband looks at his wife and says, "You know, Gladys, if you hadn't made me eat that revolting oat bran every morning, I could have had this ten years ago!"

With a few adjustments, this could be a gag about the pleasures available in old age rather than in heaven.

ON MODERATION IN ALL THINGS

An overriding theme in Aristotle's *Nicomachean Ethics* is the virtue of moderation in all things, the golden mean between excessiveness and insufficiency. As an example, Aristotle cites the virtue of courage: too much of it results in recklessness, too little in cowardice. Find the middle ground, he advises us; it makes for an all-around better life. I particularly like the idea that Aristotle ties this virtue in human behavior to an aesthetic ideal: there is something pleasing and beautiful about moderate behavior just as there is something pleasing and beautiful in an artfully proportioned object like an isosceles triangle or a well-balanced piece of architecture. Beauty is equilibrium, and equilibrium is beauty.

Like Epicurus, Aristotle has also had an influence on modern Greeks. A large proportion of them eat fatty meats, drink alcohol, and smoke cigarettes, but for the most part they enjoy these pleasures in moderation. Yes, they may choose to smoke a cigarette or two at the end of a long meal, but they don't anxiously puff on cigarettes all day long or enlist in a stressful behavior-modification program to cease smoking altogether. It is little wonder that the Greeks are among the longest-lived people in today's world; it isn't just the olive oil in their "Mediterranean diet."

ON PONDERING TRANSCENDENT
QUESTIONS IN OLD AGE

I am now sitting alone under an awning on the terrace of the sole taverna in Vlihos. Today I want to read and think a bit about some philosophical ideas that have always eluded me.

In addition to being at the perfect stage for reviewing his life, an old man is in a prime position to noodle about the "meaning of it all" questions that burned in his mind as a young man but then receded as he got down to the business of making a life for himself. (To paraphrase John Lennon, life is what happens while you are philosophizing about its meaning.) But now these questions feel significant again; in fact they feel more urgent than ever.

For all his negativity about old folk, Aristotle did say that "education is the best provision for the journey to old age," and part of what he meant is that acquiring good tools for thinking—and thinking philosophically—prepares us for one of the principal callings of an authentic old age: pondering the big questions.

I need to take a step back when considering such questions. Sometimes I think my basic philosophical impulses, those "what's it all about?" churnings in my gut, were ruined by studying academic philosophy. Too often I became preoccupied with the heady, abstruse concepts of the great thinkers and lost that sense of wonder that made me read them in the first place. I need to remind myself that to head off in the direction of philosophy, a person really only needs the basic intuition that the unexamined life doesn't quite cut it for him.

ON TAKING PHILOSOPHICAL
RISKS IN OLD AGE

In the comedy film *The Bucket List*, two terminally ill old men compose a list of experiences they want to have before they kick the bucket, and they then set off to have them. High on their list are skydiving, climbing the pyramids, going on an African safari, and, for one of them, visiting a high-priced call girl. The idea is that they have nothing to lose at this point, nothing to fear, so why not go for it? For my part, I can go to my grave regret-free without doing any of those particular things, but the spirit of their adventures speaks to me. I have nothing to lose or fear by taking some philosophical risks at this point in my life.

When Epicurus said that our minds gain a unique freedom in old age because of our "absence of fear for the future," among other things he was saying we can now take mental risks that were too scary for us when we were younger. And taking some philosophical risks—say, the one Camus famously dared us to take when he wrote, in "The Myth of Sisyphus," "There is but one truly serious philosophical problem and that is suicide"—is almost as scary as jumping out of an airplane fastened to a flimsy-looking canopy. Come to think of it, these risks are pretty closely related: they both demand us to stare death straight in the face. Kierkegaard pulled no punches when he challenged us to take philosophical and spiritual risks; he famously wrote, "To dare is to lose one's footing momentarily. To not dare is to lose oneself."

ON DARING TO THINK ILLOGICAL
THOUGHTS IN OLD AGE

Here in the Vlihos taverna, with people seated around me, I pull Heidegger's *Introduction to Metaphysics* out of my shoulder bag. This is the tome that opens with the stupefier, "Why are there things that are rather than nothing?"

Whatever could have possessed me to lug this baby across the Atlantic to this remote island village? It must have been the inevitable thoughts of mortality that hover over me. Heidegger's question seems to go beyond the start and stop of an individual life—say, mine—to *being* itself. What is that all about?

I have this nagging suspicion that for the past fifty-odd years I have been dismissing Heidegger's question as total twaddle without ever really trying it on for size. Martin Heidegger was a twentieth-century German existentialist who focused—if hundreds of pages of dense, enigmatic prose can be called a focus—on the concept of being. As much as I can grasp his question, I gather that he is *not* asking why some things exist and others do not, or even asking what it is that causes something to exist and what constitutes its existence. No, he is after even bigger game than that. Heidegger is asking us to confront the idea that existence itself can be called into question, and this, he believes, is the ultimate philosophical question. He writes: "To philosophize is to ask 'Why are there things that are rather than nothing?' Really to ask this question signifies: a daring attempt to fathom this unfathomable question by disclosing what it summons us to ask, to push our questioning to the very end. Where such an attempt occurs there is philosophy."

I need some retsina.

In Greece the accepted way to summon a waiter is to clap your hands loudly. I still have trouble getting myself to do this:

it feels impudent, like issuing a command to a slave. Not that Greek waiters appear to mind in the least—actually, it allows them to sit and drink on their own rather than hovering about to see if a customer wants anything or, as waitpersons in America are prone to ask, "Are you still *working* on your dinner?" I clap. I order a half-kilo carafe of the taverna's best. I sip down a few generous mouthfuls and look again at Heidegger's fundamental question.

This time around I am struck by a couple of things that had not penetrated before. Heidegger states that the question is "unfathomable." First he tells us that this question is fundamental to all philosophy, and then he tells us that we are never going to get it anyhow. Something perverse in that.

But what about those phrases "a daring attempt to fathom" and pushing "our questioning to the very end"? Is Heidegger suggesting that simply *raising the question*, grappling with the idea that being itself can be subject to doubt, is some kind of end in itself? I am reminded of Aristotle's observation, "It is the mark of an educated mind to be able to entertain a thought without accepting it." Might this also apply to entertaining a question that most likely has no conceivable answer?

When I was in college, I chuckled smugly about Heidegger's fundamental question. In those days—the 1950s and 1960s— we were all enthralled by the school of philosophy known as logical positivism and its sister, linguistic analysis. Philosophers like Bertrand Russell, the young Ludwig Wittgenstein, and A. J. Ayer brought logic, mathematics, and the scientific method to bear on the big concepts of metaphysics and ethics, and found them wanting. Concepts of good and evil? Nonsense! They have no rational basis, so forget about them. We only consider questions that have logical content and solutions.

Heidegger, of course, was not spared, starting with that "why" in his basic metaphysical question. The positivist Paul Edwards argued that there is a "logical grammar" to the word "why" that Heidegger violates in his question, therefore his question is meaningless. Next question?

But my schoolboy mind-set existed once upon a time, very long ago. As an old man, I am somehow able to entertain ideas that violate the logic of grammar. Of course, one reason for that may be that I am already going soft in the head. It has been known to happen. But on the other hand, in old age I do seem to be able to get occasional glimpses of ideas that appear to transcend logic. I *dare* to think illogical thoughts. So for the moment, at least, I'll cut Heidegger some slack.

ON ALTERED CONSCIOUSNESS IN OLD AGE

The midafternoon sun has just found me where I have been hiding under the taverna awning. It blasts my eyes, and for several seconds I keep staring at it, allowing it to dazzle my brain.

When I was a little kid, my brother used to tease me about

my practice of lying on my back on my bed, staring at the naked lightbulb that hung from the ceiling of our bedroom. All I could say in my defense is that I liked the way it made me feel. I believe this was my first taste of "getting high."

Not long after college, my friend Tom and I experimented with psychedelic drugs. It was, after all, the sixties. But I like to think that we were more under the influence of one of our favorite philosophers, the nineteenth-century American pragmatist William James, than our infamous faculty member Timothy Leary. James was fascinated by altered states of consciousness and considered nitrous oxide (a.k.a. laughing gas) his drug of choice, no less than a door to the Hegelian absolute, the ultimate truth. In *The Varieties of Religious Experience*, James wrote, "Sobriety diminishes, discriminates and says no; drunkenness expands, unites, and says yes."

Tom and I were reaching for our ultimate *yes*. A good gander at the Hegelian absolute would have been nice too. Alas, it was not to be. At least, if either of us did glimpse anything meaningful way out there in yes land, we were unable to bring it back home.

But now, staring into the Aegean sun, I *do* feel a little brain tickle. The retsina doesn't hurt. "Why *are* there things that are rather than nothing?" Crazy question. What would total nothingness be like? What if the sum total of everything was zero? It boggles the mind to even consider the idea of universal nonexistence. It goes far beyond the idea of human mortality; it is asking what it would be like if there were nothing and no one to be perishable *in the first place*. And, maddeningly, why it turned out *not* to be that way.

Perhaps it is impossible to get one's head around immutable nothingness: the mind just keeps collapsing in on itself. I can only barely get the idea of subtracting everything from the universe. But an eternal nothingness to which nothing could possibly be added escapes me. Maybe the positivists were right, after all: the reason I cannot think about this stuff is because it is utter nonsense.

But what's this? For an instant, I feel something like relief or even gratitude that being *is*. I even experience tinges of something that feels a wee bit like awe—awe that miraculously being has somehow triumphed over nothing. And that, astonishingly, I have been a part of that triumph: I have had the privilege of participating in being and of being conscious of that fact.

And that is it—my yes! moment. It is over in a minute, and it was not even a full yes—more like a shiver of assent. I now realize why I wanted to be around people for today's philosophical skydive. Like the "minder" who kept a watchful eye on us when we took our LSD trips, to make sure we did not follow up on our "insight" that we could fly from a third-floor window, my fellow denizens of the Vlihos taverna are my ballast. For better or for worse, they keep me from flying so far yes-ward into the realm of mind-boggling philosophical abstractions that I will never come back. Maybe I have not been so daring after all.

Nonetheless, I feel remarkably gratified by my little mind excursion. I feel enriched, in part because I have trod where I dared not tread as a young man. The old man has mellowed to metaphysics.

The best remedy for anger is delay.

——SENECA

Chapter Six

Iphigenia's Guest

....

ON STOICISM AND *OLD* OLD AGE

....

I have hitched a ride on a train of donkeys carrying supplies to the monastery at the top of the mountain overlooking Hydra's harbor. Like Pavlos on the lead donkey, I sit sidesaddle on my mount, clinging with one hand to a wooden saddle-strut. I am probably too old for this, but it is delightful. Although I am only three feet higher than when I walk this stony path, this donkey-top view is utterly new: my eyes are now level with the first-floor windows of the houses we pass, and I shamelessly peer inside at dioramas of domesticity.

At frequent intervals, and without missing a step, the four

donkeys ahead of mine drop grassy turds. A new law to placate sensitive tourists requires donkey men to stop, sweep up the lumps, and carry them to a suitable resting place, but Pavlos does not comply. He has horticulture on his mind. As a reward at the end of their workday, donkeys here are fed a tea made of poppy petals, and local folklore has it that in only one day's time a new poppy will germinate from every unloaded donkey stool. Indeed flowers are pushing out of virtually every crevice along our way. I like to think that Pavlos has an innate reverence for the circle of life.

Pavlos lets me off halfway up the mountain. From here, I walk a narrow path to a grand nineteenth-century ship captain's villa that now serves as the island's old people's home. My landlady, Iphigenia, works here. This morning I volunteered to pick up the mail in the port post office and, seeing that Iphigenia had received a long-awaited letter from her daughter in Australia, I decided to bring it to her so she wouldn't have to wait until the end of the day to read it. I've also been curious to see this place.

A man in his eighties or nineties is sitting on a bench next to the villa's courtyard gate. His chin rests on his folded hands, which, in turn, rest on the top of a wooden cane in front of him. I say, "Good afternoon," in Greek, but he does not respond. I nod to him in the tilted-head Greek way, but he does not respond to this either.

The gate is open; I call Iphigenia's name, and a few moments

later she meets me, flushed and surprised. When I hand over her daughter's letter, she is delighted, but she stuffs it into her apron pocket, saying that she wants to read it leisurely after she finishes preparing Spyros's coffee. With a nod of her head, she indicates that Spyros is the man on the bench.

"The others don't want coffee?" I ask.

Iphigenia smiles. "Spyros is the only elderly person who does not have family on the island," she says. Apparently the legislators in Athens who established this palatial old folks' home did not take into account that no self-respecting Hydriot son or daughter would deny his aged parent a bed and care in his own home. Spyros is the villa's sole occupant.

As it turns out, Spyros requires a great deal of care. He is senile and incontinent and given to frequent fits of anger and despair. Iphigenia does her best, never leaving the villa until Spyros, fed and bathed, is asleep in his bed.

I cannot help wondering how much longer I have before I become like Spyros. Senility and incontinence are what we have to look forward to in *old* old age. It is abominable. As Shakespeare described it, among his "seven ages" of man, this

> *Last scene of all,*
> *That ends this strange eventful history,*
> *Is second childishness and mere oblivion,*
> *Sans teeth, sans eyes, sans taste, sans everything.*

That stage of life is coming up next for us old folks, whether or not we choose to be conscious of it.

ON THE PRINCIPAL CAUSE OF DEPRESSION
IN *OLD* OLD AGE

In Susan Jacoby's chilling investigation of today's increased longevity, *Never Say Die*, we learn what modern medical science, at great expense, has largely given to us: extended years of decrepitude. Whereas in days of yore a late-in-life heart attack or stroke would finish us off, we are now given stents and bypasses and cups full of meds, which essentially bring us back from death's door. At first look, this seems fine and dandy. Except the result of our expanded life span is that diseases like Alzheimer's and Parkinson's assault us at an ever-increasing rate in these "bonus" years. Our bladders fail, our limbs tremble, and our energy dwindles to just above vegetation. Locked inside our decaying brains and bodies, we become isolated from everyone and everything we ever knew. Alive is the new dead.

A burgeoning specialty in gerontology is geriatric depression. Nursing homes now employ psychiatrists, psychologists, and social workers to deal with this rapidly growing problem. Professional periodicals like the *Journal of the American Geriatrics Society* publish innumerable articles on such topics as how to properly administer the Geriatric Depression Scale and which antidepressants have proved most effective with the "end-of-life population." Psychiatrists, of course, regularly weigh in with their estimates of the principal causes of this depression.

Principal causes? I believe I could give these psychiatrists a helping hand on that question: it is because *old* old age stinks. It is horrible. The quality of life is usually zero. And if we still have any rational powers left at that point, we know that life is only going to get worse. This makes it difficult to see geriatric depression as a mental disorder. It seems more like an authentic and fitting response. These gerontological psychiatrists would have pumped Dylan Thomas's father full of Effexor if he had followed his son's exhortation to "Rage, rage against the dying of the light."

ON RAGE AND STOICISM

God knows, I can all too easily get into raging against the dying of the light. The entire prospect of gradually and inevitably falling apart, with death as the only possible relief, not only fills me with terror, it overwhelms me with anger. Not fair, any of it. This is the final payoff for having lived a long and fruitful life? Who made the rules? I hate it, all of it.

But what can come of my rage? Even if it feels authentic to cry foul in the face of this ultimate cosmic joke, is howling with fury the way I want to spend the period of my life before *old* old age gets me? The Stoics, both Greek and Roman, would certainly argue against taking the rage route.

Stoicism, founded in Athens by Zeno of Citium, not long before Epicurus took up residence there, developed over the course of more than three centuries, reaching into all regions of Greece and to Rome, where such philosophers as Seneca and Marcus Aurelius refined and elaborated upon its fundamental tenets. This philosophy's most abiding idea is that people should liberate themselves from their passions and surrender uncomplainingly to what is unavoidable, because dwelling on what is out of our control invites pain without any conceivable gain.

Zeno out-Zenned Epicurus in his prescription for a calm and comforting happiness; he advocated fully detaching ourselves from our desires rather than, as Epicurus proposed, calibrating and mapping out various routes to contentment. Epictetus, a first-century Greek, succinctly expressed the results of practicing Stoic philosophy: "Show me one who is sick and yet happy, in peril and yet happy, dying and yet happy, in exile and happy, in disgrace and happy. Show him me. By the gods I would fain see a Stoic."

The Stoics, then, would advise us to cut loose at the very source of our rage against the horrors of *old* old age by becoming *indifferent* to *old* old age's claim on us. After all, it is out of our control anyhow. With no expectations or desires, we will experience no geriatric depression.

I do not think I am able to do that. Sometimes the practice of Stoicism feels more like denying pain than transcending it, and denial of any kind has rarely seemed to me like an authentic way to live. (There are also times when the practice of Stoicism seems like a mind game, one that comes perilously close to singing to oneself "Don't Worry, Be Happy.") But one compelling idea that I do take away from Stoic philosophy is the business about letting go of matters over which I have no control. Focusing on the horrors of *old* old age before I get there would get me nowhere. For starters, it would be a waste of precious and very limited time.

ON ENDING LIFE BEFORE IT
BECOMES WORTHLESS

Still, there is one question about upcoming *old* old age that cannot be postponed: when is it no longer meaningful to remain alive?

The Confucian philosopher Mencius put the situation simply and eloquently when he wrote, "Life is what I want; *yi* [often translated as 'meaningfulness'] is also what I want. If I cannot have both, I would rather take *yi* than life. On the one hand, though life is what I want, there is something I want more than life. That is why I do not cling to life at all cost. . . . In other words, there are things a person wants more than life and there are also things he or she loathes more than death."

The Roman stoic Seneca put it even more bluntly in one of his collected letters to the Roman governor of Sicily, Lucilius:

"Life has carried some men with the greatest rapidity to the harbor, the harbor they were bound to reach even if they tarried on the way, while others it has fretted and harassed. To such a life, as you are aware, one should not always cling. For mere living is not a good, but living well is. Accordingly, the wise man will live as long as he ought, not as long as he can. . . . He always reflects concerning the quality, not the quantity, of his life. As soon as there are many events in his life that give him trouble and disturb his peace of mind, he sets himself free. . . . For no man can lose very much when but a driblet remains. It is not a question of dying earlier or later, but of dying well or ill. And dying well means escape from the danger of living ill."

And as a preamble to his recommendation to end one's life before it becomes intolerable, Mr. Cheerfulness himself, Arthur Schopenhauer, wrote in *Studies in Pessimism*, "Every man desires to reach old age; in other words, a state of life of which it may be said: 'It is bad today, and it will be worse tomorrow; and so on till the worst of all.'"

Personally, I find Mencius and Seneca more sympathetic on the subject of ending life at the appropriate time.

There is no *yi* in Jacoby's account of *old* old age. Do we really want to cling to life at all costs? Do I?

ON THE PRACTICABILITY OF ENDING LIFE
IN *OLD* OLD AGE

Although both Mencius and Seneca make profound, if distressing, sense about the point at which it is better to die than to continue living, they do not offer any advice on a critical practical question: how do we know exactly when that point has been reached? The timing is tricky. We need to pull the plug *before* we cross the line into full-fledged dementia; otherwise we will be beyond the point of rational decision making, yet before we cross that line, we may still have a sufficient number of "driblets" left to make life worth living.

This is less of a conundrum if we have graduated to life-support machinery and have signed a living will that empowers a deputy to pull the plug at this point; in effect, our doctor takes care of the timing problem the moment he decides we need to be attached to (and, hence, detached from) a ventilator. But this is a special case, as is the situation of being in intractable pain that no medicine or amount of time will relieve. It is not difficult for someone to decide to finally end that pain the only way possible rather than continue to endure it for the rest of his life. In my wife's country, Holland, unbearable, untreatable pain is sufficient reason to ask for and be granted physician-assisted suicide.

But what if we are still able to breathe sufficiently and are not in intractable pain, yet the quality of our lives has been reduced to zero? The probability is that at that point we will not have the wherewithal—the rationality or the strength—to put an end to "living ill." And asking someone in advance to make that decision for us—even after presenting her with a detailed list of circumstances and conditions that define the point at which we want to be "set free"—often comes to naught. In the end, relatives and friends may understandably lack the will to make that decision. We are left with our own calculations and predictions.

—⁓—

I have a curmudgeonly old friend named Patrick who has dubbed this period of our lives "waiting for the diagnosis." Which upcoming day or doctor's visit is going to deliver the news that our first major geriatric, and possibly fatal, disease has shown up? Needless to say, Patrick is not an adherent of Stoic philosophy.

Nonetheless, he is correct in his assertion that a fatal disease *will* show up eventually; only *when* remains incalculable. Well, not entirely incalculable. Researchers at the University of California have compiled a number of geriatric prognostic indices that allow us to plug in our stats—age, gender, body-mass index, personal medical history, etc.—and, voilà, out pops our life expectancy. It is, of course, just a ballpark figure, but still a statistically significant one. In terms of medical care, this provides a calculus for determining, for example, whether it makes sense to get another colonoscopy or mammogram; if, according to the indices, we will in all probability die of something else before colon or breast cancer can substantially damage us, the sensible course of action is to skip the test and save time, discomfort, and expense.

This life-expectancy index may also serve as a guide to the Mencius/Seneca puzzle: when to plan and execute our final exit. But for some reason I don't feel like doing the math on that one just yet.

ON ANTICIPATORY DEPRESSION IN OLD AGE

Watching Iphigenia spoon-feed coffee to Spyros in the courtyard of the old people's home, I again find myself thinking about my friend Patrick. He is not yet in *old* old age. His is not geriatric depression; it is *anticipatory* depression: he knows what is rapidly coming down the pike, and it makes him bitter and morose. He tells me that I am as unauthentic as any forever youngster, that my quest for an authentic old age is ultimately no different from the forever youngster's relentless busyness: we are both in denial of what is coming our way any day now.

Could Patrick be on to something that I have ignored? Could Aristotelian old-age grumpiness be the most personally honest way to go? The old man as curmudgeon has a long tradition, including as a comic stereotype in plays and movies. He reflexively grumbles that "they" don't do things the way they used to, which, of course, was the *right* way to do things. Most younger people believe the grump is actually griping about the fact that he is so out of date that he has outlived his usefulness. Come to think of it, that *is* worthy of some serious grumbling.

Turning into a curmudgeon may have its perks. Before my departure for Greece, Patrick said to me, "Bitching about getting old has become my favorite pastime. Actually, it's my new raison d'être." Hey, it works for him.

But not for me. I remain with Plato's older brother, Glaucon, when he says, in the *Republic*, "But to me, Socrates, these complainers seem to blame that which is not really in fault. For, if old age were the cause, I too being old, and every other old man, would have felt as they do. But this is not my own experience."

My existentialist head cannot help wondering why Patrick's anticipatory depression has not been his "authentic" attitude toward his life all along. After all, we have known since we were quite young that the end of life—especially if we lived a long time—wouldn't be any fun. Does this mean that if we did not plunge into utter despair at the age of twenty-one, we were in total denial? In the scheme of a finite life, how much difference can there be between fifty years and five years until that inevitable and sorry final stretch?

The existentialist Albert Camus certainly thought despair was an authentic response to the apparent meaninglessness of life, let alone to the horrors and sicknesses that await us in *old*

old age. But Camus also believed that we can transcend life's inherent absurdity and create meaning through our own decisions and interpretations; that too is an authentic response to what awaits us. All of which is to say that perhaps authentic old age can consist of neither the breathless ambition of the forever youngster nor the unremitting despair of my friend Patrick but something meaningful in itself.

Still, maybe I haven't given Patrick's attitude its proper due. Contemplating Spyros's vacant stare and quivering lips, it *is* difficult for me to keep my own anticipatory depression at bay. As Aristotle mercilessly noted, there is absolutely nothing to look forward to in *old* old age.

As for me, I guess the best way I can keep myself from being preoccupied with the despair of impending *old* old age is by heeding my takeaway lesson from the Stoics, that focusing on the horrors of *old* old age before I get there would be a waste of the time I have left. With so little time left on this side of that final stage, I don't want to spend it dwelling on what is clearly beyond my control. I simply would rather try to figure out how to spend this time in the best possible way.

ON THE HIDDEN PERILS OF ROMANTICISM

Walking back down the steep and rocky path toward the port, I realize the time has come for me to acquire a cane of my own, at least for precarious treks like this one. This idea makes me smile.

Although I have never been much of a shopper, I find myself looking forward to picking out a cane. One with a pewter caryatid on top, like Tasso's? Or something less elegant and more practical, with a simple curved handle?

Ahead of me is one of the many "pocket" cemeteries scattered on the hills of Hydra. I stop, wondering if it would be disrespectful to walk through it as a shortcut. I have always found Greek cemeteries oddly consoling; it is their modesty, I think—plain, body-length stone slabs with simple headstones that often contain a glass-covered, fading photograph of the deceased. Now I spot, at the far end of the cemetery, a string of donkeys bent down to munch on poppies. Just behind the animals, I see the back of an old man seated alone on one of the horizontal gravestones, and I can hear him talking animatedly. I am pretty sure that it is the donkey man, Pavlos. He must be chatting with a lost loved one. His late wife? I wonder if he does this regularly—review his day with his lifelong partner as he did when she was alive.

I tread as quietly as I am able inside the cemetery, my eyes straight ahead. I do not want to intrude. And then, from the corner of my eyes, I catch a glimpse of Pavlos's face: he is talking on a cell phone!

I am not only disappointed, I am chagrined. Over the years, more than one of my friends has accused me of romanticizing the Greeks and their way of life. These friends certainly seem to have got it right this time.

But hold on—I can now make out that Pavlos is chatting with his granddaughter, something about a beautiful dress that her aunt is making her for Easter. Pavlos is completely and delightedly into this conversation. He is relishing this happy interlude in the cemetery. My romantic imagination had not grasped the half of it.

A little philosophy inclineth man's
mind to atheism, but depth in philosophy
bringeth men's minds about to religion.

———————

—FRANCIS BACON

Chapter Seven

The Burning Boat in Kamini Harbor

A fire flares in the sea just beyond Kamini Harbor. Cheers rise up from the people crowded at the water's edge and reach me on my terrace. It is the evening of Greek Easter, and the blaze is the traditional burning of Judas in effigy on a raft.

Reflected off the rippling dark water, the flames create a dramatic effect—exciting, festive, yet there is something in the tenor of the crowd's cries that is distressing, a mobbish overtone of vengeance, of "Burn, baby, burn!" It does not sound holy to me.

In his screed *God Is Not Great: How Religion Poisons Every-*

thing, the late social commentator Christopher Hitchens cataloged the ways in which organized religion corrupts us, turning the world into an agglomeration of vindictive mobs. He wrote that whether in "Belfast, Beirut, Bombay, Belgrade, Bethlehem or Baghdad . . . I would feel immediately threatened if I thought that the group of men approaching me in the dusk were coming from a religious observance."

I certainly do not feel threatened by the revelers in Kamini's bay; nonetheless this is one Greek shindig I think I will sit out. Like Hitchens, I believe organized religion "ought to have a great deal on its conscience."

But this does not stop me from yearning for a spiritual dimension to my life, although I am not clear what that would mean.

ON OLD PEOPLE AND THE GOD DELUSION

Old folks often turn toward religion. It was always so. In our current psychologically minded era, the accepted reason for this is that old people can hear death knocking at the door, so as a coping mechanism we redouble our efforts to cook up a god and a hereafter.

In his seminal essay *The Future of an Illusion*, Sigmund Freud categorically dismissed religion as simply a product of our wishes. Interestingly, and perhaps even bravely, he wrote the essay near the end of his life. In it, he argues that religion has the principal purpose of controlling society and enforcing a moral code by promising a reward for one's ethical conduct on earth *after life is over*, thereby guaranteeing good behavior right up to the end. It is a neat thesis. Currently, evolution theorists and geneticists are giving this theory a fascinating new spin with their speculation that a "religion gene" exists. That gene expresses itself in a group survival characteristic, and tribes without this gene died out because, without a compelling religious moral code, they killed each other off. Obviously, Christopher Hitchens would have taken issue with the idea that religion is a survival characteristic.

Freud's assumption is that if ideas such as a transcendent god and a lovely afterlife come into our minds merely as a result of our *feelings*, then they must be nonsense. At a strictly logical and empirical level, as Sportin' Life sings in *Porgy and Bess* apropos the dicta of the Bible, this assumption "ain't necessarily so." For example, our feelings could be the sole source of our idea that the stranger in a fedora hat sitting across from us in a train is a serial killer, but it could turn out that the guy in the fedora actually *is* a serial killer. That we came to this idea in a nonrational way has no bearing on whether or not it is actually and independently true.

Piling on the psychological interpretation of why we cook up God are today's new atheists, philosophers like Sam Harris and Richard Dawkins. These thinkers point out that most of us subscribe to scientific, logical-empirical thinking in 99 percent of what we do, but then we go off the deep end into illogical, nonempirical thinking when it comes to God and religion. We pick between the two ways of thinking according to what we need: a scientific head suits driving a car, while an illogical, nonempirical head is a better fit when it comes to praying for salvation.

Sam Harris puts it amusingly: "If I told you that I thought there was a diamond the size of a refrigerator buried in my backyard, and you asked me, why do you think that? I'd say, this belief gives my life meaning, or my family draws a lot of joy from this belief, and we dig for this diamond every Sunday and we have this gigantic pit in our lawn. I would start to sound like a lunatic to you. You can't believe there really is a diamond in your backyard because it gives your life meaning. If that's possible, that's self-deception that nobody wants."

At the basis, this is another "to thine own self be true" argument: either we believe the scientific model for determining what is real or we don't. Self-servingly flip-flopping between the two is just a way of kidding ourselves, being untrue to ourselves.

Are we old people who turn our attention to spiritual matters just kidding ourselves? Are we willfully being untrue to ourselves simply because we "hear Time's winged chariot hurrying near"?

ON THE TIMELINESS OF SPIRITUALITY
IN OLD AGE

The Hindus certainly do not think we are being untrue to ourselves. They believe we old people are simply finally ready to get down to serious spiritual business.

This ancient South Asian religion and philosophy has its roots in the Iron Age, with its "modern" development beginning in the second century BCE. Like most enduring philosophies that address the question of how to live, Hinduism marks out distinct roles for different stages of life; it lists four: *brahmacari* (student), *grihastha* (householder), *vanaprastha* (forest dweller or hermit in semiretirement), and *sannyasi* (the renounced one). Respectively, these stages represent periods of preparation, production, service, and spiritual contemplation. Some Hindu texts suggest that the final stage usually commences after the seventy-second year of life. I can relate.

What I find both startling and compelling about this final stage is that high on the list of things an old man renounces is religion itself. The ceremony initiating the *sannyasa* period includes burning copies of the sacred Hindu text, the Vedas, a symbolic rejection of all the religious beliefs and practices the *sannyasi* acquired in his earlier stages of life. Good-bye to all that. The old *sannyasi* is completely on his own now. Through solitary meditation, he has to find whatever spiritual enlightenment he can. In effect, if he is going to have religion, he needs to reinvent it from ground zero.

The renounced one's life makes living simply in Epicurus's garden seem like retirement in Sun City. *Sannyasis* are wandering hermits, living without shelter or possessions. They only eat when food is given to them. Still, there is a resonance between Epicurus's idea of a totally free life and the Hindu's fourth stage.

Describing the *sannyasi* life, the "Asrama Dharma" says: "The *sannyasi* has his spiritual eye on goods that men can't give and cares little for anything that men can take away. . . . Therefore, he is beyond the possibility of either seduction or threat." And in another section: "Business, family, secular life, the beauties and hopes of youth and the success of maturity have now been left behind. Eternity alone remains. And, so it is to that—and, not to the tasks and worries of their life, already gone which came and passed like a dream—that the mind is turned."

I am certainly familiar with the feeling that my "already gone" life "came and passed like a dream." All too often it feels like it went by in the blink of an eye. And I also get a feel for what the "Asrama Dharma" is talking about when it says, "Eternity alone remains." I am in the final conscious stage of life, and increasingly my mind is drawn toward the search for what the Hindus call "the true wisdom of the cosmos."

The Hindus remind me that the psychological explanation is not the only way of accounting for why we are drawn toward spiritual matters in our old age. The renounced one is not seeking enlightenment because he is caught up in some system of rewards and punishments in the hereafter, and not even because he fears death. He has kissed all those concerns and anxieties good-bye. Rather, now that he is done with the business of life and his connections to worldly affairs, it is time for him to finally focus on the ultimate spiritual questions.

ON ONE OLD MAN'S QUEST FOR
SPIRITUALITY

Religion has not played a significant role in my life to date. And I do not find much consolation in the fact that the *sannyasi* starts off with a blank slate too; even though he has rejected the religious training of his youth, I suspect that he begins his journey with a stronger sense than I have of what enlightenment might look and feel like.

Still, my inchoate yearning for some kind of enlightenment is clearly there. I believe it has always been. Indeed I suspect that it is always there—*somewhere*—in most of us. Maybe I am being soft in the head again, but my guess is that deep down even the most rabid atheist has a hankering for a transcendent dimension; he just cannot get a believable bead on it. As for me, I simply have gotten into the habit of ignoring my spiritual yearnings, as if they were some kind of annoying tic. I am like the man who, when admonished by Baba Ram Dass to "be here now," replied, "I'm cool—I am definitely planning on living in the present *any day now.*"

But again, the unique urgency of old age chastens me: if not now, when?

The fundamental questions at the root of spiritual yearnings are not difficult to identify; it is just hard to make meaningful sense out of them: Do I have any kind of connection to everything else? To the cosmos? Are we both—the cosmos and I—in this thing together? And if so, what does that mean about how I should live the rest of my life?

Questions do not get much vaguer than these do, yet it is difficult to think of questions that are more essential. After my bout with Heidegger's "unfathomable question" the other day, I feel better equipped to wrestle with the new atheist's claim that I would be untrue to myself if I even entertained the idea of a spiritual dimension. I do not think I am searching for a *thing*, like Sam Harris's mythical diamond the size of a refrigerator in my backyard. I do not expect to see the face of God or the landscape of heaven. It is some sort of sublime understanding I am after, an existential assent to the universe. Again, it is the philosopher William James who gives some hope to my yearning: no, I am not looking for a *thing*; I am searching for a spiritual *experience*.

And so I return to James's *Varieties of Religious Experience*, another favorite old book of mine that I've brought along on this sojourn. Indeed, the copy sitting on my desk in Hydra now is the same one I bought at a Harvard Square bookstore some fifty-plus years ago, my earnest student underlinings and marginal notes still intact. One passage I underscored back then speaks directly to what I am musing about now: "We pass into mystical states from out of ordinary consciousness as from a less into a more, as from a smallness into a vastness, and at the same time as from an unrest to a rest. We feel them as reconciling, unifying states. They appeal to the yes-function more than to the no-function in us. In them the unlimited absorbs the limits and peacefully closes the account."

Yes, it is a jiggle of my "yes-function" that I am seeking. And if I have such an experience, I will take it from there. If Harris informs me that the experience was merely a wish fulfillment, I will take that under advisement. But I reserve the privilege of rejecting Harris and embracing my yes.

— ⧟ —

For the likes of me, I do not think eternity can be sought in the way the *sannyasi* does, by focusing everything I have on the mysteries of the cosmos. To be honest with myself, I am not really willing to give up my life as a "householder," especially the part about giving up my house. I know that it is just such bourgeois attachments as this one that may be keeping me from transcending the material world, so if my attachment to home and hearth means I do not sufficiently yearn for enlightenment, I guess I will have to accept it. In any event, I doubt that enlightenment would come to me by focusing on it the way I imagine the *sannyasi* does. I wouldn't even know how to begin to do that.

What is more, I do not think going to services at a synagogue or church will get me there either; it never has before. And unlike William James and Aldous Huxley, my drug trips merely managed to get me to the anteroom of nirvana, not all the way through the doors of perception.

So what is this old man to do about his last chance at spiritual enlightenment?

—m—

I find myself thinking again about Plato's belief that pure play has intimations of the divine. And again I vividly recall that enchanted night when I witnessed five old Greek men performing their exalted dance to life. To me, it was a glimpse into the transcendent. This exaltation in life is, in the end, one religion I can believe in. But glimpses such as that one come all too rarely.

My ninety-year-old friend Henry, a retired professor who was widowed last year, recently phoned me with a problem he was having. Although his mind is still working well, and his body functions adequately, he is nonetheless considering moving into a retirement home for the companionship. The problem, he said, was his music. He listens to classical music upward from four hours a day, often at high volume, and he does not want to be told by anyone to turn it down; furthermore, he doesn't like earphones because he thinks they distort the sound.

I had to laugh. I know how much music means to Henry, especially at this point in his life, and I am absolutely sure sacrificing just one minute of listening time even for a good conversation just would not be worth it for him.

Henry insists that he is not a spiritual man. He says religion is just hocus-pocus. And yet when we go to a symphony concert together—which is usually one with Mahler on the program—and I glance over at him, I often behold on his creased old face an expression of rapture. Henry is clearly elevated to a higher realm—his spirit soars. I have no doubt that in some meaningful sense Henry has left the building.

I too listen to music more and more. Throughout my life, music has stirred me more than any other art form, and now, in old age, I find myself listening to it almost every evening, usually alone, for hours at a time. Lying on the couch in the dark, listening to, say, Mahler's Ninth Symphony or the Fauré Requiem or Puccini's "E lucevan le stelle" from *Tosca*, I too sometimes take off for a realm where self-consciousness and my separateness from everything in the universe fall away. I am lost in the stars. Like Henry, I am hesitant to name this a spiritual experience, but at times it feels awfully close to one. Eyes closed, breath stilled, listening to the exquisite melancholy of Cavaradossi's *romanza* to Tosca under the stars as he awaits his execution crying out, "Never have I loved life more!" sometimes—just sometimes—I can feel my yearnings made sublime.

And what about those all-too-rare moments when a glimpse of sky or a leaf dancing in the wind suddenly plucks me out of my day-to-day consciousness and sets me floating in some transcendent kingdom? Are these enough to answer an old man's spiritual yearnings? And is there any way I can make them more of my daily life?

I guess all I really know how to do is to be *open* to enlightenment, wholly alert to it in my head and heart. Zen Buddhism teaches mindfulness as the path to enlightenment. Mindfulness has several meanings, some considered ineffable, but fundamentally it appears to mean full consciousness, a continuous, clear awareness of the present moment. A mindful person is fully engaged in what he is presently doing—be it walking, pondering, or simply breathing. And he is ever on guard against slipping into everydayness, that is, losing full consciousness or numbing himself to it. In my old age, freed from one of my chronic "mad masters"—reflexive skepticism—I may finally be able to do that.

One of my favorite William Blake poems, "Auguries of Innocence," begins:

> To see a World in a Grain of Sand
> And a Heaven in a Wild Flower,
> Hold Infinity in the palm of your hand
> And Eternity in an hour.

Perhaps I am most likely to find the answer to my yearnings that way, by being here now—*fully* here now.

ON THE HOLINESS OF THE ORDINARY

The pungent aroma of roasting lamb pervades my terrace. The Greek name for Easter, Pasha, is derived from the Hebrew name for Passover, Pesach, and the paschal lamb that was sacrificed during the first Passover feast celebrating the Jews' liberation from Egypt. Greek Easter and Passover are also related by the dates on which they fall each year: both are calculated by the phases of the moon. Lamb is always the main course for Easter dinner in Greece.

I am having dinner tonight with Tasso and Sophia at their home. A few days ago, as Tasso was leaving his group of friends at Dimitri's taverna, he stopped at my table and asked me if I had plans for Easter dinner. When I said I did not, he insisted that I join his family for the feast.

Before I knock at the door to Tasso's courtyard, I rehearse my greeting, "Kalo Pasha!" (Good Easter to you); as a Jew, even if a nonpracticing one, I feel more comfortable with that than with the alternative Greek Easter greeting, *Christos anesti!* (Christ is risen!). I then primp up the bouquet of field gladiolas I picked on this morning's walk. I knock, and Tasso opens the door.

"Kalo Pasha!"

"Kalo Pesach!" Tasso replies and he embraces me.

Did I hear that right? Did Tasso say, "Good Passover" to me?

He did indeed. I am convinced of it by the sparkle in his eyes. And when his lovely, white-haired wife, Sophia, appears behind him, and I present her with the flowers, she too says, "Kalo Pesach!" Clearly, she has rehearsed her greeting too.

In this moment, I realize the depth of lovingness in my dinner invitation. I am certain that Tasso anticipated my discomfort with the boisterous burning of Judas in the bay. In fact I am sure he understood my sensitivity to it better than I did myself: it did not just spring from my generalized Christopher Hitchens–like antipathy to the corrupting influence of organized religion; it came from my knowledge—Tasso's and my knowledge—that hatred of the betrayer, Judas, often contains overtones of anti-Semitism. What an incredibly compassionate man Tasso is. *Christos anesti*, indeed!

Tasso and Sophia's son, Kosmas, and Kosmas's wife and teenage son are here too, in from Athens for the holiday. Like Tasso and Sophia, they are warm, welcoming, animated people.

The leg of lamb is still roasting on a spit over an open fire in Tasso's garden. After all, it is only nine in the evening, far too early for the main course of a Greek dinner on a warm spring night. First, ouzo and mezes, a seemingly endless parade of plates containing grilled octopus, toasted cheeses, pork sausages spiced with orange zest, olives, stuffed grape leaves, cucumber and yogurt salad, on and on. The cook for each of the mezes proudly passes his specialty around the garden, announcing his personal touch—for Kosmas's son, Nikolaos, it is the mint leaves he stirred into his eggplant salad.

Toasts are made: to Niko for passing his college-qualifying examination; to Kosmas's wife, Despina, for publishing a poem in an Athens magazine; to Tasso and Sophia's aging dog, Cybele, for surviving another winter. Cybele is named after the ancient goddess of nature, and this is the only tribute that has a reference to anything remotely theological. Neither Jesus nor the Resurrection is mentioned, nor, for that matter, is Moses or the parting of the Red Sea.

For devout Christians, what is happening in Tasso's garden represents a corruption of religion. Easter has lost its meaning here. They are removing the divine Resurrection from this holy day and replacing it with a profane holiday party. Even if I had not been invited, I am pretty sure Tasso's feast would have skipped religious testimonies and gestures.

But sitting here, under a budding lemon tree, among these lively, loving people, I am absolutely certain that Tasso's garden is alive with something essentially holy. I see it in the warm glances exchanged around the fire. I hear it in Kosmas's tender teasing of his father for his habit of depositing olive pits in his shirt pocket. I feel it all around me.

I owe much of my appreciation of what is happening here in Tasso's garden to my age. As an old man, I am at peace with this peacefulness. There is nothing I want from these people except their companionship. There is no new excitement or accomplishment I long for. Indeed at this moment there is nothing more I want from the cosmos than I have right here: "to see a World" in their faces.

This must be what old Epicurus felt at his long table of

friends in the Garden—the sublimity of being among good people. I find myself suddenly missing my wife and daughter more acutely than I have in the entire month I've been away. I wish I could be sharing these blessed moments with them.

And now I remind myself that I must heed William Blake's warning not to attempt to cling to a sublime experience, but rather allow it to come and go with grace. In another of his metaphysical poems, the four-line jewel called "Eternity," he writes:

> *He who binds to himself a joy*
> *Does the winged life destroy;*
> *But he who kisses the joy as it flies*
> *Lives in Eternity's sunrise.*

I stand and raise my glass. "It is a great privilege to be here," I say. Then, smiling, I add, "In fact, it is a great privilege simply to be."

Take more time, cover less ground.

———————

—THOMAS MERTON

Epilogue

Returning Home

....

ON A MINDFUL OLD AGE

....

The pale green hills outside my window offer a soft contrast to the piercing landscape I have left behind. I am home in our small wooden house in Western Massachusetts, sitting at my study's desk, with my Hydra notebooks in front of me. Across the hallway, my wife, Freke, is working on an article for a Dutch magazine. My dog, Snookers, snoozes at my feet.

For the first few days of my return, I did little but talk with Freke; we had a month's worth of stories stored up. We chattered happily for hours on end. Coincidentally, while I was away,

Freke's editor in Amsterdam had sent her down to Florida for several days to investigate a new American phenomenon: old people who return to work for financial reasons. The Dutch "hook" was that in Holland retirement at age sixty-five is mandatory for everyone.

Some of the oldsters Freke interviewed in Florida said that going back to work exhausted them. Many had taken jobs less interesting than the ones they had in the prime of their lives, and they found this disheartening. Yet a good number of them confessed that they could "make do" on their pensions but were unwilling to downgrade their living accommodations and general lifestyle to do so. I wondered if these people might take a lesson from Epicurus—scale down and enjoy the leisurely pleasures of old age.

Yet Freke also told me that many of these old folks said they were reinvigorated by being back in the workplace. It felt good to be a productive member of society again; it was gratifying simply to be busy. One oldster said she felt like she had "come out of seclusion."

As it happened, on my last day in Kamini, Dimitri handed me an article, from the Greek news blog Ekathimerini. It described how a good number of Greek pensioners—many of whom were still waiting for their pensions from their bankrupt government—had returned from Athens to their home villages in Crete, where they had taken up farming. One was quoted as saying, "Here you can go a week without spending a single euro. You get fresh food from your farm and if you need something extra, like olive oil for example, you can get it from a fellow farmer." This man, and many others, sounded delighted with this surprising turn in their lives in old age. It is tempting to say that they have serendipitously unearthed Epicurus's garden.

~

One problem with philosophical thinking—as with most academic disciplines—is that it tends to stick ideas into absolute categories, leaving little wiggle room for the complexities and inherent internal contradictions of ordinary human experience. One of Aristotle's lasting contributions to philosophy and science was his counsel, "We must not expect more precision than the subject-matter admits." And the question, "What is the best way to be an old man?" is far from being a precise one. In fact it's about as open-ended as they get.

Maybe Epicurus's rather dogmatic prescription for happiness—to first and foremost free oneself from "the prison of everyday affairs and politics"—simply does not correspond to what makes many old men and women in America today genuinely happy. To be true to oneself, a person needs to make his own decisions about what brings him happiness. Indeed if I am going to be true to myself, I have to ask myself what I think I am doing here at my desk, with my notes spread out in front of me, at the age of seventy-three. Clearly, I think I still have some work left to do.

Is there an acceptable golden mean between the "forever young" ethos and the Platonic/Epicurean/existential ideal of a fulfilled and authentic old man? Can we split the difference without compromising both extremes so much that we end up with a mushy philosophy of old age?

Could it all come down to something as mundane as how we schedule our remaining time? Say, work twenty hours of the week and devote the rest of our time to these essential last-chance old man's endeavors? But that way, wouldn't we inevitably be reentering a "schedule mode" of existence, complete with time limits? And once we have opted for that mode, even if we have scheduled time for playing with our friends (and dog) and reflecting on our past, we will still have one eye on the clock, forsaking the rich and luxurious "lived time" of an unhurried old man.

—⁓—

For hours now, I have been reviewing my Hydriot notebooks and trying to decipher my marginal scribbles in my philosophy books. My notes to myself alternately strike me as simplistic and compelling, occasionally both. I find myself feeling like Guido in *8½*: "Everything is just as it was before. Everything is confused again, but this confusion is *me*!" I cannot help wondering if my quest for a relevant philosophy of authentic old age was nothing more than a befuddled old geezer barking at the moon.

But just maybe there was something faintly Heideggerian in my quest. Clumsy as it was, maybe it was "a daring attempt to fathom" the "unfathomable question" of what makes a good and gratifying old age. Perhaps simply raising the question has been some kind of end in itself.

ON GROWING OLD MINDFULLY

Maybe that Buddhist notion of mindfulness will lead to the most valuable way of living a good and authentic old age. Perhaps whatever we do, we must try to remain mindful that we are old: that this is the last stage of life in which we can be fully conscious, that our time in this stage is limited and constantly diminishing, and that we have extraordinary opportunities in this stage that we never had before and will never have again. Perhaps if we are as mindful as we possibly can be of where we are in life right now, the most fulfilling options of how to live these years will reveal themselves to us, not by rigorously following the prescriptions of the wise philosophers, yet by being ever mindful of their wisdom.

By simply being aware of the old-age options that men like Plato, Epicurus, Seneca, Montaigne, Sartre, and Erikson examined and commended to us, we can make authentic choices for how we want to conduct this period of our lives. We can try their ideas on for size, see how they fit with our considered values. This may be what it means to grow old philosophically.

—⁓—

Out my study window, I see that my wife is now sitting in an old wooden chair by the garden. She has a manuscript in her hands, but she is not reading it; she is gazing lazily out at the pale green hills. I leave my notebooks scattered on my desk and go out to sit next to her. I now realize that a request has been twitching in the back of my mind for several weeks now—a request I wish to make of her and our daughter and some of my friends.

"I think I need your permission to become an old man," I say.

She laughs, of course. "My permission? What for?"

I laugh too. "I don't know. I guess I think you'd rather I stay young or at least *try* to stay young."

"Permission granted," she says, smiling. "Anyway, I think it's too late—that sounds like an old man's question."

ACKNOWLEDGMENTS

I very much appreciate the valuable help of family, friends, and colleagues in putting together this manuscript: my daughter, Samara Klein, who offered me organizational ideas I would not have come up with on my own; my old pal Tom Cathcart, always a better student than I, who spotted mistakes in my reasoning and gently guided me out of them; and my wife, Freke Vuijst, who, in her second language, respectfully improved my syntax and grammar.

As always, Julia Lord, my agent and friend, not only supplied me with good advice, but, even more important to me, encouragement. My editors, Stephen Morrison and Rebecca Hunt, were wise and patient critics through many drafts. I am grateful.

I also appreciate the help of my friend Tician Papachristou, a generous tutor on all things Greek, and the travel companionship of my buddy Billy Hughes, whose photographer's eye often opened my own eyes.

Finally, I am deeply grateful to my Hydriot companions—Tasso, Dimitri, and, of course, Epicurus.